GOD ANSWERS SCIENCE

Gary Driver

Copyright © 2018 by **Gary W. Driver**

All rights reserved. No part of this publication may be reproduced, distributed or transmitted in any form or by any means, without prior written permission.

All scripture quotations, unless indicated otherwise, are taken from the King James Version of the Bible.

God Answers Science/Gary W. Driver. – 1st ed.

ISBN: 978-0-9852783-5-9

Table of Contents

Preface vii

Chapter 1 | Is God Dead? 1
    Origin 3

Chapter 2 | The Greatest Second in Time 7
    The Beginning, Time=0 7
    Space-Time, 10^{-43} 11
    Energy, 10^{-43} 14
    Information, 10^{-43} 17
    First Language, 10^{-43} 19
    Starting with Laws, 10^{-43} 24
    Flat Universe, 10^{-36} 28
    Inflation, 10^{-36} 35
    Higgs Field, 10^{-12} 36
    Elementary Particles, 10^{-12} 41

  Initial Conditions, $10^{-43} \sim 10^{-12}$...............43

  Cosmogony—Before the Beginning...............44

Chapter 3 | Between Genesis 1:1 & 1:2...............49

  Simple Elements...............49

  Dark Matter—Creator's Dust...............51

  Stars...............57

  Galaxies...............63

  Galaxy Clusters...............65

  Expansion of the Universe...............66

  An Accelerating Universe...............69

  The Immeasurable Universe...............74

Chapter 4 | The Days of Our Solar System...............81

  The First Day—Hadean Eon...............89

  A Star Is Born...............96

  The Second Day—Archean Eon...............102

  The Third Day—Proterozoic Eon...............105

  Plate Tectonics...............109

  The Fourth Day—Proterozoic End...............116

  The Fifth Day—Phanerozoic Eon...............121

  Mass Extinctions...............126

  The Sixth Day—The Cenozoic Era...............134

  Adam and Eve 146

  The Seventh Day 152

Chapter 5 | Sustainer 157

  Entropy 163

  Thermodynamic Entropy 166

  Educational (Information) Entropy 168

  Economic Entropy 170

  Entropy for Life 171

Chapter 6 | Ecology of Earth 175

  Make It Rain 175

  Thunder and Lightning 183

  Paths of the Sea 189

  The Flood 196

Chapter 7 | Omni-God 205

  The End of the Universe 207

  Evil 210

  The Unknown God 218

  Faith 222

Amen 229

Preface

What do you think when you look to the majestic night sky? Where did it all come from? How did you originate? If you've ruminated over these questions, you're in good company. For thousands of years, humans have puzzled over these mysteries, even though answers have been hard to come by.

Many have limited themselves by looking only to science or religion. Ironically enough for both camps, it is the Bible that points us in the right direction. It instructs to "lift up your eyes on high, and behold who hath created these things" (Isaiah 40:26a). Stargazing will not yield answers; rather, the scripture instructs us to investigate with vigor, through the discipline of science.

On the other hand, science is limited to the natural world, which cannot create itself. And we are tired of hearing each side shout from their towers. Einstein put it this way: "I cannot conceive of a genuine scientist without that profound faith. The situation may be expressed by an image: science without religion is lame, religion without science is blind."

Modern landmark scientific discoveries like general relativity, the accelerating and flat universe, the Higgs field, plate tectonics, and the first second of creation along with the seven eons of Genesis, and many other phenomena, are found in the Bible. The intent of this book is to show the faithful that science will increase the foundation of their faith in God as Creator and show the skeptic the Bible has answered science before science knew how to ask.

Chapter 1

Is God Dead?

We live in a unique time in human history as it relates to the knowledge of our universe and how it works. Modern precise instrumentation and computer technology, working in tandem with the vast body of accumulated knowledge, have opened many doors to expand this understanding. Yet many questions remain.

From our early history, humankind has gazed into the night sky and marveled at its beauty and mystery. Until about four hundred years ago, our vision restricted our ability to comprehend the immediate world around us, and the distant cosmos. Many natural phenomena were merely attributed to a plethora of deities.

Throughout history, knowledge gradually increased and revealed the natural causes of many of these phenomena. Many deities were disproven and lost their influence. This inverse process of rising knowledge and declining deities continued. The very scripture even proclaimed, "the secret things belong to God" (Deuteronomy 29:29). But the number of mysteries decreased as science progressively unlocked them. The mysteries became known as gaps in the knowledge of phenomena. The applying of God to the mysterious gaps became a term of derision known as "the God of the gaps." As far back as the nineteenth century, even Nietzsche famously declared, "God is dead."

Fast-forward to 1966 when *Time* magazine published its famous cover entitled, "Is God Dead?" This highlighted the questioning of the foundation of the core beliefs of Christians, which included the influence of scientific knowledge. In the twenty-first century, still others have suggested God is a delusion and the universe has no need for a Creator. In the documentary *God and the Scientist*, Professor Colin Blakemore of Oxford University makes a rather bold statement about the God of the Bible, proclaiming, "Science is the biggest challenge that Christianity will ever have to face." Later in the documentary, he accuses anyone who considers God as a viable answer to knowledge of being ignorant and unlearned.

In spite of this noisy, anti-theistic dogma, history shows that many scientists have ignored the noise to acknowledge God and use their knowledge to bring about great scientific discoveries—luminaries such as Galileo Galilei, Sir Isaac Newton, Johannes Kepler, Nicholas Copernicus, Michael Faraday, Max Planck, Blaise Pascal, Maria Mitchell, Gottfried Leibniz, Georges Lemaître, Erwin Schrödinger, George Washington Carver, Werner Heisenberg, Lise Meitner, George Stokes, Lord William Kelvin, Percy L. Julian, Sir Francis Bacon, René Descartes, James Clarke Maxwell, Robert Boyle, Charles Hard Townes, Louis Pasteur, William Harvey, William Herschel, Andrew Pinsent, James Joule, and even the deist Albert Einstein. Indeed, God and science can reside in the same brilliant, productive mind.

Just as Jesus waited to visit his sick friend Lazarus until the appointed time, as outlined in John chapter eleven, God waited to reveal himself as Creator starting in the twentieth century with the discovery of an expanding universe that had a beginning, both of which the Bible proclaimed thousands of years ago. Contrary to "the God of the gaps" assertion, the revelation in this book uses major discoveries in science as evidence God is Creator. Scattered throughout the Bible are once-hidden descriptions of major scientific phenomena that chart the chronology of creation from the very beginning to the death of the universe, answering the challenge of modern science of the last four hundred years. By the end of this book, the question on the famous April 1966 *Time* cover will be answered persuasively. As Marcello Truzzi said, "Extraordinary claims require extraordinary evidence.[1]"

Origin

The origin of existence is one of humanity's most vexing questions, but science has made significant progress toward finding an answer. Physics have pinned down the creation of the universe to an infinitesimal amount of time after the creation event generally called the Big Bang. The problem is that the laws of physics are the only vehicles available, and it breaks down near the Planck wall. The Planck wall is a hypothetical barrier used to represent the shortest measurable time duration after the Big Bang, a fraction (10^{-43}) of a second after creation.

To simulate the extreme conditions of creation, scientists have used particle colliders with ever-increasing energy capacities. Today, the largest ever built is called the Large Hadron Collider (LHC), located in both France and Switzerland and spanning some seventeen miles in circumference. However, the physical road to the origin of the universe will end at the Planck wall, along with physical existence and the opportunity for experiment.

This great accomplishment was achieved by thousands of scientists from around the world. Most valiant research contributions have gone unnoticed because they were carried out, at times for decades, as experiments for a myriad of theories that failed. This

---

[1] Marcello Truzzi. "On the Extraordinary: An Attempt at Clarification," *Zetetic Scholar*, Vol. 1, Number 1 (1978): 11.

foundational work of elimination paves the way for the Nobel Prize awards for great discoveries by the few.

In spite of these great accomplishments, no one knows what occurred beyond the Planck wall to the actual start of creation. Perhaps a theory that unifies general relativity and quantum physics will expand this. At this point, our knowledge of a theory beyond the laws of physics is mere conjecture. Once the Plank wall is penetrated past the beginning, we are confronted with nothing.

Nothing—nonexistence in the absolute sense; the absence of anything and everything, including space. Nothing has no cause, no interest, no value, and no consequence. Nothing is a metaphysical concept, totally out of the arena of natural science—the total absence of the physical.

Space-time, a vacuum, undifferentiated potential, quantum fluctuations, and the fundamental forces are all something, *not* nothing. Therefore, even in the empty black void of space, there was still something: the Higgs field and the physical laws governing that perceived emptiness. Nothing is as difficult to conceptualize as infinity. Only nothing was before time. Any natural existence constitutes time, requiring a creation event. Before time, nothing of the natural universe existed.

However, just because humankind cannot grasp the full meaning of the literal emptiness of nothing does not make the concept of "nothing" impossible. Some attempt to change the meaning of "nothing" to allow for a creation theory, like the random fluctuation in a completely empty void that needs nothing to be "something" in order to support the existence of a natural cause for creation. This proposed change of the meaning of nothing changes everything. Consider, if nothing was actually changed to something, what will "something" now mean? Something and nothing, by definition, simply cannot have the same meaning.

This forces something to become anything! The conundrum continues because something cannot have the same meaning as anything, which induces another forced move to make anything be everything. Of course anything and everything are also not equivalent! The final act of this madness is when everything is kicked out of space to become absolutely nothing. Thus, changing the meaning of nothing is no simple task; it also requires changing the meaning of *everything*!

From ancient times, "nothing" was considered to be outer space. Even in recent times, space was believed to be void of anything. Now we know space contains substances such as elementary particles and fields. Out of nothing, the universe was created. The word "beginning" in Genesis 1:1, the first verse in the Bible, is translated from the Hebrew word *re'shiyth,* which means "first." First is the number one, and what comes before one? Zero, nil, zilch, nada, naught. Everything had to be created from zero, even the quantum world of elementary particles, dark matter, and fields. Before the beginning, there was nothing; this is the concept of creation from nothing.

The start of creation from the "real" nothing means the laws of physics cannot emerge from a point before they existed. To address the beginning of the universe, we must consider an entity that is greater than the natural world that transcends space and time. The first cause of creation must be greater than time itself to be considered a first cause because nothing is greater in the natural world than time. Let's begin with the first second in time and examine the Bible to see if God can answer the great efforts of science in his claim as Creator.

Chapter 2

The Greatest Second in Time

The Beginning, Time=0

> In the beginning God created the heaven and the Earth. (Genesis 1:1)

Nothing in nature is eternal; everything has a beginning. The beginning of creation is the start of time if we look at time in a classical sense. It is the first physical event. The Big Bang is a name given to the very beginning of creation often described as an explosion, like a bomb. However, the Big Bang was an extremely rapid expansion of creation. According to the Standard Model of cosmology of the universe, the universe has a beginning, as the Bible proclaimed some three thousand years ago. Cosmologists cannot claim to know the age of the universe and deny it has a beginning. No single scientific discipline, including physics, can describe the entire workings of the universe. Before the physical world existed, physics did not.

The beginning of the universe is the highest degree of order that has ever existed. Entropy is considered to be the constant flow to disorder from the greatest possible order, starting from 10^{-43} of the first second of time. The process of entropy started at creation and grew from there.

Creation is, strangely, an event of extreme order from nothing. The image below is called the Cosmic Microwave Background (CMB) radiation. It is an image of the actual temperature of the afterglow in the microwave spectrum resulting from the Big Bang. Scientists theorize this radiation or light was released approximately four hundred thousand years after the Big Bang. The temperature variation is evidence of the smoothness and order that took place at creation. The temperature fluctuations between the lighter spots and the dark spots are approximately one part in one hundred thousand of a single temperature degree across the image. This uniform temperature is an extreme amount of uniformity across the visible horizon estimated to be ninety-six billion light years. It confirms the Big Bang was a great expansion, not an actual explosion.

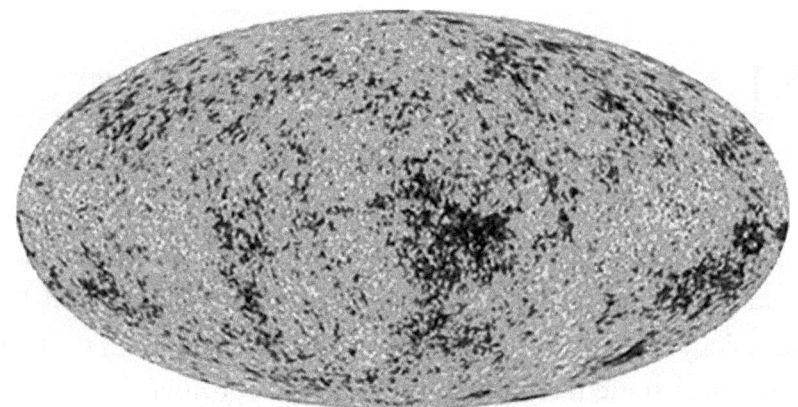

NASA-Cosmic Microwave Background Radiation Image

Increased genera follow all ten mass extinctions

In the 1500s, Copernicus, a church deacon, introduced the concept of a heliocentric system, in which the planets revolve around the sun. This was contrary to the long-held belief among scientific *and* religious folk that the sun and planets revolved around Earth. This new discovery of the heliocentric system turned the old concept of how the universe operated on its head.

Similar to the old belief that the sun revolves around Earth was the long-held belief that the universe had always existed and had always been the same, termed the Steady State model of the universe. But eventually, this model, too, was refuted.

In 1929, even with the discovery of an expanding universe by Edwin Hubble and others, the Steady State model of the universe remained the predominant theory. Before Hubble's discovery, Einstein's theory of general relativity postulated the existence of an expanding universe. The theory of general relativity describes the geometric characteristic of gravity for the macroscopic universe. For a time, even Einstein rejected his own conclusions and held to the Steady State model. Despite decades of observations indicating the universe was expanding and dynamic, most scientists clung to the Steady State model until the 1960s.

One problem with a universe with a beginning was its resemblance to the biblical account of creation. However, the discovery of the CMB radiation in the 1960s, along with the previous discovery of an expanding universe decades earlier, served as a one-two knockout punch to the long-held concept that the universe is static and eternal in its origin. In other words, the universe had a beginning.

It was a tough pill for some to swallow because it was empirical proof of what the Bible foretold in Genesis 1:1, back in 1500 BC. It took humans thousands of years to reach the same conclusion via advanced telescopes, instrumentation, computers, and advanced mathematics. Without using a single instrument, the God of the Bible declared in ancient times that the universe had a beginning. The scribe who is credited with the writing of Genesis is Moses, who had no scientific knowledge on which to base his writing. Moses's source was a revelation, not a handed-down story.

In Moses's day, only a few were able to read and write. Moses himself was educated in Egypt, in Pharaoh's house. But even an erudite man like Moses could not have been the source of this cosmic knowledge. At the time of the writing of Genesis, only by firsthand knowledge could these things be known. However, the only way to have firsthand knowledge was to have been present at the event that occurred before humankind, or the universe itself, existed. Thus, the greatest claim ever known was made, that God is the Creator of the universe.

The notion that the universe had a beginning and was not simply "always there" is only one of numerous facts the Christian Bible discusses concerning the creation of the universe. In the course of this book, we will look at other such predictions that affirm the God of the Bible is Creator.

From everlasting (before the start of time), God had a plan. A claim for causality that posits God as Creator generally leads to a common question: from whence did the Creator come? No one knows where God came from, but that does not negate his existence or what he has done. It is merely one of many unanswered questions. The causality question of what caused God is the start of an infinite regress of causes (i.e., if God was caused by some other cause, what caused *that* cause? And then what caused *that* cause in turn?) To ask a question to which we do not know the answer does not negate the existence of empirical evidence that might answer other questions. As with any other test of causality, we can know one answer without knowing the original or preceding cause or causes.

For example, we know who created the Eiffel Tower, but how many of us know who created Eiffel? Because we cannot come to a consensus about Eiffel's creator (not his parents), we are not handcuffed in determining who created the famous tower in Paris. Therefore, not knowing if or how God came to exist does not prevent us from determining, through empirical evidence, the entity that created the universe out of nothing. The testing of God's declarations about the universe made in the Bible will be affirmed via empirical data and the observations of modern science.

This book takes a chronological path from the beginning of creation to the present age and brings out the things the Bible says concerning creation. It seeks to prove that the author of the Bible is indeed the Creator of the universe. The Bible has numerous claims about creation phenomena, and the only way to verify them is through empirical science.

Forensic evidence is scientific evidence of what has occurred. As in a murder trial, we will examine the scientific evidence to conclude if God indeed is the "culprit" who created the universe. Just as a common person is capable of serving on a jury to make a determination of guilt, we do not have to be scientists to render a verdict on creation.

Space-Time, 10^{-43}

To go from nothing before creation to something (energy) requires space. Space is also something in and of itself. Newton characterized time and space as a backdrop or stage on which all phenomena occur, an analogy that is not complete but correct. Time as a whole is omnipresent and immutable; no experiment can be done outside of time. Time's complete dominion over all physical phenomena was established fully at the moment of creation, to be the director of the stage of the universe, thus keeping everything moving in the "future" direction called the arrow of time.

Individual time is experienced differently as special relativity declares. Special relativity is a theory by Albert Einstein that describes the characteristic of time measurement between two observers, one stationary relative to the other moving near the speed of light. And gravity indeed affects time as outlined in general relativity. Time, as a whole, dominates all of creation to keep all things moving from the past to the future.

As part of the greatest second of time, the Creator made predictions about the characteristics of space at a time when humankind considered space to be nothing. From the beginning of time itself, space had to be created. The first event in creation marks the beginning of time. What we observe today is what Einstein revealed in his theory of special relativity, a space-time continuum, which means that space and time are intertwined so that they affect one another in a local way.

Even today with the aid of computer graphics and animation, it is difficult to explain space. The Creator used the metaphors of the biblical era to describe his predictions about the characteristics of the heavens, including space. Most scientists today use the metaphor of two-dimensional fabric to describe three-dimensional space, just as the Bible describes it. Thousands of years ago, the Bible predicted space was indeed something, and that it clothed everything. Scientific observations from the smallest to the greatest components have confirmed these predictions. Like clothing, which contours to that which it clothes, space contours all mass.

> I clothe the heavens with blackness, and I make sackcloth their covering. (Isaiah 50:3a)

This biblical statement concerns the heavens or "the universe," the term used today. Everything in the universe is both clothed and covered with the fabric of space. Modern science also uses the fabric metaphor to describe the characteristic of space. This scripture actually contains two metaphors that have a common reference to the *fabric* of space: clothing the heavens and covering the heavens with sack*cloth*. The word sackcloth is translated from the Hebrew word *saq*, meaning a mesh sack. These two metaphors are analogous to fish in water. The fish is *clothed* with scales and is *covered* with water.

I will first deal with the clothing metaphor. What comes to mind if you were asked to cover a rock on a table with fabric? We tend to see a rock with a cloth on top of it. Contrary to that perception, the rock would be covered entirely as if we are in deep space without a reference to up, down, or any other direction. This is how to consider the references to this scripture: the entire three-dimensional surface of everything, from elementary particles to the largest object in the universe, is clothed with the blackness of space.

The only objects we see with the natural eye in the heavens are those that give off light, such as stars, galaxies, and comets. Likewise, in this first clothing metaphor of Isaiah 50:3, an observer would peer into the night sky and see the vast blackness we call space covering every object. And if the observer were not in an illuminated area, the blackness would also clothe him or her better than a wetsuit, even while on Earth.

The word translated as blackness is a unique word, unlike many of the commonly used words representing darkness or evil in the Bible. In this scripture, "blackness" is translated from the Hebrew word *qadruwth*, meaning black, which is used in the Bible only this one time. In this scripture context, the heavens are doing exactly what the Creator has commanded via the laws of physics, which he established. This special word represents the blackness of space, which hugs and moves with the objects it covers just like clothing or fabric.

Space is not nothingness; it contains particles, matter, energy, and fields. God would not need to clothe the heavens with space if space was actually nothing. If the scribe were writing based on humankind's limited knowledge of the natural world, he would have declared space to be nothing or empty and would have eventually been proven wrong by modern science. Observations confirm space actually clothes everything, even that which we cannot see, and it has the characteristic of fabric.

Energy, 10^{-43}

> For the invisible things of him from the creation of the world are clearly seen, being understood by the things that are made, even his eternal power and Godhead; so that they are without excuse. (Romans 1:20)

The context of this scripture is the creation of the world or universe, and the invisible things that originated from the Creator at the time of creation. The invisible things are the different forms of energy from the creation of the universe. Time, space, and energy are the beginning of natural creation. From a physical standpoint, scientists can explain how the universe developed from today back to what is termed a singularity based upon the laws of physics.

This invisible, abstract phenomenon called energy manifests in many forms throughout the universe, as through the basic forces of gravity, electromagnetism, the strong and weak nuclear force, along with potential, kinetic, electric, mechanical, chemical, thermal, and other types of energy. Energy in all its forms and quantity came from the initial creation of energy.

Despite its many uses and various methods used to measure it, energy is hard to define. Energy can be observed, measured, calculated, and even regulated, but what is it really? The most common definition for energy is "the ability to do work." Approximately 70 percent of the universe is in the form of dark energy, which came from the original common quantity of energy of creation. Like the energy forms that we handle and use every day, dark energy is an invisible mystery.

Increased genera follow all ten mass extinctions

How can an invisible existence at the beginning of creation be clearly seen as the scripture declares? The word "clearly" is translated from the Greek word *kathorao*, which means "to see physically" and "to perceive or understand." This verse also declares this invisible mystery is understood by the things that are made. This phrase refers to the workmanship of the Creator, in accord with the original claim of Genesis 1:1 by the God of the Bible, that he is the Creator of the universe. The workmanship of the Creator is quite a vast statement, referring to all that is contained in the universe—every atom and elementary particle that exists.

The mystery of energy is clearly seen in a different form called mass. Today, mankind understands the energy-mass equivalence, better known as $E=mc^2$. And we understand it by all things made of mass. We can see and understand that the invisible energy and mass are one and the same. Throughout time, mankind could clearly see the invisible energy in the form of mass, but it wasn't until Einstein discovered its equivalence that we have come to understand it.

In the above scripture, the word "power" is translated from the Greek word *dunamis*, which means "strength, power, and ability." From the invisible God, *all* power (energy) in the universe, regardless of form, originated at creation. In the first part of this verse, this energy/mass phenomenon is claimed to come from God himself; thus, having some attributes of God. Two of the attributes of God that are manifested in energy are its inherent power and invisibility. The third attribute of God manifested in energy/mass is its eternal essence. This is the basis for the first law of thermodynamics: energy can be transformed from one form to another, but cannot be created or destroyed. This attribute of energy is a testimony of God, in that he cannot be created or destroyed. He is the first cause, and uncreated Creator, of the universe.

The word "Godhead" in the last part of Romans 1:20 is translated from the Greek word *theiotes*, which means "divinity" or "divine nature." Occurring in the Bible only here, it is unique in its description of the Creator as being above the natural world in order to have created it, having authority over all. Being divine and thus greater than nature, God's power is the source of creation itself. We experience invisible time, invisible space, and invisible energy in everyday life. By observing the time, space, and energy phenomena with which we interact on a daily basis, we have no choice but to recognize the Creator's divinity and his hand in creation.

Energy has the attributes of God himself:

- *Of him – From God himself*
- *Invisible – God is invisible*
- *Indescribable – God is indescribable*
- *Source of all natural life – God is the source of all life*
- *Eternal in essence – can't be created OR destroyed – God is the same*
- *Source of all natural power – God is the source of all power*

Energy is not from the eternal past, as it was created at the beginning with time and space. Since they must be created themselves, time, space and energy cannot be considered as first causes. The first cause is the entity that caused all things to come into existence. The first cause cannot be natural in its essence because all natural things must be created by an uncreated entity. According to the Standard Model of cosmology, at the initial creation there is only energy, which the Bible declares comes directly from the Creator. The first law of thermodynamics limits any natural thing or entity from creating energy. Hence, energy cannot create itself. The finite amount of energy in the universe at creation is the same amount there is currently, though diluted in an ever-expanding system.

Without this uncreatable, invisible, and controllable entity called energy in the universe, nothing would exist, move or function; therefore, we can consider energy as the second cause. The laws of physics govern the second cause, energy, being abstract; the laws are not the creative first cause. If energy (second cause) is from God as it is stated in Romans 1:20, by numerical reduction, God is claiming to be the first cause. Energy, being the second cause, must come directly from the first cause. The Industrial Revolution was driven in large part by an expanded knowledge of the laws of physics and their applications, giving humans the ability to direct energy in its many forms to do work. To this day, energy is defined by its ability to do work—yet no one knows what it *really* is.

Information, 10^{-43}

Information is a very important part of creation from the instance of the Big Bang. To describe and comprehend space, time, and energy requires *information*. Information is inherent in all physical existence from creation. Before an artist or craftsman gathers materials and tools to accomplish a task, they must use their imagination to visualize the end product that will be produced. This imagination is packed with information. Even a camera cannot take a picture (image) without gathering information and placing it on the film or storing it digitally. Imagination is an abstract concept, yet it contains information.

The Creator spoke about creation information in the following scripture. This describes the changing of the imagination of God into the reality of invisible elementary particles, which is the essence of all creation.

> Through faith we understand that the worlds were framed by the *word* of God, so that things which are seen were not made of things which do appear. (Hebrews 11:3)

Information is represented by the use of "word," which is translated from the Greek word *rhema*, which means "to utter words" or "speech." All speech is the transfer of information. By the word (information) of the Lord, the worlds were framed (fitted). The information contained in speech originates from the mind of the speaker, which implies the information necessary for the universe came from the Creator. The scripture follows the reference to information by stating all that can be seen is made from things that cannot be seen, which describes the actual instructions of the framework of the universe. The unseen things of which all matter (worlds) is made are elementary particles. The framework of the universe is quantum mechanics. There are other scriptures that use "word" with different context and meanings. For instance, Psalm 33:6-9, uses the Hebrew *dabar* in reference to the authoritative command or fiat of God as Creator. In addition, John 1:1 uses the Greek word *logos* in reference to the written record of scriptures, which both directly and indirectly reference Jesus.

Just as humans can have a plan in their mind, God can have a plan for the universe before the start of creation. Even in its uncertainty, the subatomic world of quantum mechanics contains information to be atoms and to become molecules, just as DNA contains information of its essence, and instructions by which living creatures are to develop and function. This information did not need conscious humans for its existence.

Information is organized knowledge and instruction that applies to space, time, energy, physical laws, and forces at creation. The information that can be accessed within fractions of the first second of the universe's existence must have existed before creation. That means there was a place for it to be organized and called information in the first place. No artist, architect, or craftsman can bring a non-idea to fruition.

Consider the amount of information that scientists use to model cosmological theories of how the universe was formed.

Take, for example, the Lambda cold dark matter or Lambda-CDM Big Bang cosmological model, the Standard Model of the universe. Scientists use computer simulations to model the formation of the universe from the first moments to its current state. Coupled with observations and experimental findings, the model has been refined to obtain a progressively more precise understanding of what has taken and what is taking place in the universe.

The amount and complexity of information required are reflected in physicists' use of the world's most powerful supercomputers to simulate the beginning, processes, and growth of the universe. The supercomputer called the Cosmology Machine (COSMA) is located at the Institute for Computational Cosmology (ICC), one of nine research institutes at Durham University, England. The simulation is rerun with different physics until it matches the physics of the observed universe.

First Language, 10^{-43}

> Philosophy is written in that great book which ever lies before our eyes — I mean the universe — but we cannot understand it if we do not first learn the language and grasp the symbols, in which it is written. This book is written in the mathematical language, and the symbols are triangles, circles and other geometrical figures.[2]

Information is necessary for mathematics to function. Wherever there is mathematics, there is information. The universal language of mathematics is the foundation of all science, and physics is the

---

2 Galileo Galilei. *The Assayer (Italian: Il Saggiatore)* (as translated by Thomas Salusbury, 1661), 178.

foundation of other sciences. The laws of physics are known and communicated by the matching language of mathematics. Humans did not create mathematics; we merely discovered it, in the same vein as the elements were discovered. The elements are the fundamental base for the chemical working of the physical world. However, the elements are tangible and undeniable, whereas mathematics is abstract and undeniable. The chemist can analyze complex compounds by understanding the characteristics of the fundamental elements. Mathematics describes the working characteristics of the physical world. The physical world is the arbiter of what is right or wrong, and mathematics is the means of description. Mathematics was discovered by humankind, and our knowledge is still evolving, but mathematics has existed since the beginning of time, just like the laws of physics that mathematics helps us to understand.

Mathematics is the universal language used by modern, educated humans, to explain both general relativity and quantum mechanics of physics, chemistry, engineering, medicine, business, economics, and every other science. Why does mathematics explain both the subatomic world of quantum mechanics and macro world of general relativity when they are worlds apart in operation and laws? Not only does it explain the universe, it has led and continues to lead scientists to discover the unknown.

Because that which may be known of God is manifest in them; for God hath shewed it unto them. (Romans 1:19)

As outlined in Romans 1:19, the scientific method of prediction by mathematics and subsequent verification by observation and experiment is the Creator's method of revealing his handiwork. God showed it to them *before* it was made known. A famous account of this revelation before knowledge is the discovery that the universe has a beginning. In the early twentieth century, Albert Einstein hammered out the most tested theory in physics: the theory of general relativity. The mathematics declared a dynamic universe contrary to the then-common belief of an eternal static universe. George Lemaitre was able to interpret the language of mathematics to declare what it suggested: an expanding universe with a beginning. Einstein initially rejected Lemaitre's analysis. However, Edwin Hubble provided irrefutable evidence of the expanding universe through observation, using the knowledge of starlight established by astronomer Henrietta Leavitt.

This verse also clearly states that what is shown (by mathematics) is not guaranteed to be made known (by observation and/or experiment). One example of this is an account of the early twentieth century, where mathematics showed the workings of the atom, even though experiment and observation could not make it known. The account in question is with the argument of the nature of atoms among physicists. Albert Einstein helped prove atoms did indeed exist. At that time, it was a major triumph for science. Afterwards, the advancement of this field required scientists to understand the operation of the atom. The conventional physics that introduced the atom was about to be challenged by the atom's strange nature, which Newtonian physics could not explain. This is where logic and intuition take a back seat to the weird world of the subatomic, which is quantum mechanics.

Such out-of-the-box thinking by Niels Bohr, Max Born, and Werner Heisenberg yielded the Copenhagen interpretation of how quantum mechanics work. The Heisenberg uncertainty principle purports that certain aspects of the subatomic world are inherently unknowable. Thanks to the advancement of modern electronics and computers, the workings of quantum mechanics, and the electron in particular, have been shown to man by pure abstract mathematics, yet the predictability of some aspects is unknowable as the name of Heisenberg's theory asserts: uncertainty. The atom is a paradox of nature at this level. This world of unpredictability becomes orderly at the macro world.

In contrast, the macro world is solid and predictable. This macro world certainty allows us to board an airplane with the confidence that the laws of physics have not and will not change, and thus the airplane will operate in a precise, predictable manner. The Creator has and will reveal his works through mathematics, but not all things are made known even with experiment.

To subdue Earth as God commanded, He has provided the light of mathematics to lead the way to understand the world in which we live. Humans must learn the language of mathematics because any endeavor that includes numbers is part of the mathematical language. It transcends all human languages and expresses the operation of the universe. It is a core part of all education around the world.

Mathematics is yet another aspect of the operation of the universe that has not evolved. After only a fraction of a second in time following creation, there was no time or opportunity to evolve. The only evolution that has occurred in mathematics is the evolution of our understanding of it. The same goes for the laws of physics. They have not changed, even though our understanding of those laws has. That being said, the world is not all mathematics and physics. Humans are required to add what the Bible calls "wisdom" to these tools.

> The universe cannot be read until we have learnt the language and become familiar with the characters in which it is written. It is written in mathematical language, and the letters are triangles, circles and other geometrical figures, without which means it is humanly impossible to comprehend a single word. [3]

---

[3] Galileo Galilei. *The Assayer (Italian: Il Saggiatore)*, 171.

Increased genera follow all ten mass extinctions

According to physicist and Nobel Laureate Leon Lederman, symmetry dictates the laws of physics, and the laws of physics dictate to all of nature (including humans). Imagine, what is found at creation is also found in music—symmetry. There was an entity *before* and after creation dictating that symmetry.

> Symmetry is ubiquitous. Symmetry has myriad incarnations in the innumerable patterns designed by nature. It is a key element, often the central or defining theme, in art, music, dance, poetry, or architecture. Symmetry permeates all of science, occupying a prominent place in chemistry, biology, physiology, and astronomy. Symmetry pervades the inner world of mathematics itself. The basic laws of physics, the most fundamental statements we can make about nature, are founded upon symmetry. [4]

All of the energy, particles, laws, and forces needed to bring about the universe and life we see today were all present at the first second of creation. All that was needed for the formation of matter, star creation, and the dissolution of the stars into the heavier elements required for the formation of our planet and for our world to operate were there at the beginning to produce the universe. The language of mathematics has given us insight back to the very beginning of the Big Bang. Thus, the language was always there, and we merely discovered it. The Bible does not predict all phenomena of creation or the first second in particular. However, all the phenomena that were established within the first second of creation imply planning before the most awesome second of all time.

---

[4] Leon M. Lederman. *Symmetry and the Beautiful Universe.* (New York: Prometheus, 2004), 13.

Starting with Laws, 10^{-43}

One aspect of time is its role in the laws of the physical world. Newton referred to time as a stage; Einstein referred to time as a player on that stage. Time is an integral part of the laws of physics, as seen in the world's most famous equation, $E=mc^2$, requiring the velocity of light (c). Without the laws of physics, there would not be space-time, as Einstein discovered in special relativity. Nor would the curvature of space-time exist, as Einstein discovered in general relativity. If the laws of physics had not been established before the energy of the universe was released, how would that energy be "governed?" There would be no boundaries or limits. If the laws of physics were created at the time that energy was created, there is no available time for these governing powers of the universe to evolve. This means the laws of physics need to be intact at the creation event. Within this extremely limited time frame, by definition, the laws were created.

Using the observable universe of today as the model, scientists have used the laws of physics to calculate events back in time and in supercomputer simulations to understand what took place in the process of time from the very first moments of the universe. This goes back in time to a remarkable 10^{-36} second (ten million, trillion, trillion, trillionths of a second) after the Big Bang to what scientists call a singularity, where the laws of physics become unreliable. These laws must have been in effect before, or at minimum at the same time, energy and matter appeared, because the universe cannot exist in an ungoverned state. The unimaginable power of the universe at creation must have been governed by the higher power of time and the laws of physics, all of which had to have been established by yet a higher power, which is the first cause.

Increased genera follow all ten mass extinctions

> Thus saith the LORD; If my covenant be not with day and night, and if I have not appointed the ordinances of heaven and Earth. (Jeremiah 33:25)

These ordinances (laws) of heaven and Earth were appointed by the Creator at creation. These are the laws of the physical world that pertain to the entire universe (heaven and Earth). Just like the discovery of the significance of the cosmic microwave background, the many discoveries of the laws of the physical world (universe) should bring glory to the one who pronounced them before they were discovered, and knew these laws were the same in both the heavens and on Earth.

It is important to point out that the Creator used the plural form of ordinances or laws. Some scientists prefer not to call the laws of physics "laws." Some also try to separate the concept of these laws from the laws that humans have made because conceiving of them as similar would mean there is a need to have a lawmaker. However, the two sets of laws are indeed similar in principle. A human law's innate authority is reflective of the power of the human lawgiver. The innate authority of the laws of physics also reflects the power of the lawgiver, which pertains to the entire universe. Therefore, the lawgiver of the physical world must have authority on the scale of, and over, the universe. There is no denying the scale of the laws of physics, and the highest intellectual creature on Earth cannot alter them. They are immutable, just like the galactic lawgiver.

Time duration has presented a revelation in the first fraction of a second of creation. The advent of the four forces (the strong force, weak force, electromagnetism, and gravity) and the laws of physics within a fraction of a second, reveal that they could not have evolved into being. Within one-trillionth of a second after creation, there was simply not enough time to evolve. The claim of planning before the creation event is necessary even for the Creator of the universe. The beginning of time is the start of the universe, not a starting point for the Creator to begin planning. The Creator of time and space cannot be subject to time and space.

Evolution is simply change over time, which has occurred from the beginning of creation. The basic meaning of evolution is at the core of the Bible. From Genesis to Revelation, the Bible proclaims change throughout time and into the future. However, this is not an undirected change. The physical laws govern but do not direct the physical world. Thermodynamics govern energy, but it is humankind that directs the energy to do work. The work of energy to bring about change is not undirected.

> Knowest thou the ordinances of heaven? canst thou set the dominion thereof in Earth? (Job 38:33)

In the Book of Job, after Job has challenged God's actions related to Job's suffering, God responds in a sarcastic manner. God asked Job to offer his wisdom concerning his creation. In Job 38:33, God asked Job if he could "set the dominion" of the ordinances of nature only on Earth.

The first problem is that no one, including Job, knows natural laws exist. The Creator makes it known that the laws have designated dominions. This is analogous to a kingdom. A kingdom is the area of rule or domain of a king. The Creator is saying that the laws have specific areas in nature in which each governs. This is evident in all physical laws and the four fundamental forces of nature that divided into distinct forces in the first fraction of a second at creation. The dominions are listed below on this graph showing the estimated time when they began to separate into their respective dominions.

Increased genera follow all ten mass extinctions

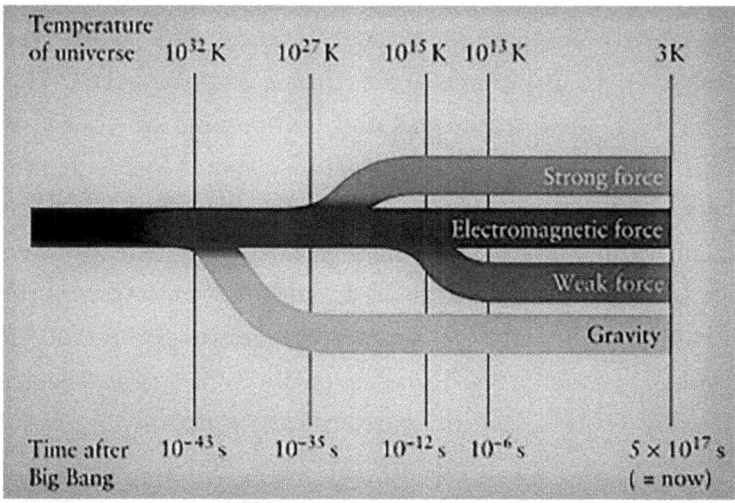

Four Forces of Nature

- GRAVITY – mass's effect on space-time
- STRONG NUCLEAR FORCE – nucleus of atoms
- WEAK NUCLEAR FORCE – radioactive decay
- ELECTROMAGNETIC FORCE – holds atoms together and charged phenomenon

The dominion of the four fundamental forces was set early in the first second of creation and according to observations remains that way today. So, the prediction or statement of the Creator to Job has proven to be correct. These appointed designated dominions hold true for all the laws of physics.

These dominions further keep in the Creator's designated strengths and perimeters with extremely precise lines of demarcations. While the differences in strength between gravity and the other three forces are great, so are the scales of their dominion, comparing the subatomic of strong and weak nuclear forces to the galactic gravitational force. In addition, the Higgs field and dark energy are tuned to be weak to properly interact with the weak gravitational force for the development and maintenance of the universe. All this to insure dominions do not overlap.

Therefore, the Creator was and is directing the course of the universe using the laws of physics and physical forces he created. These laws did not create themselves. From pure energy to elementary particles, from mass to stars and galaxies, the generation of the elements of the universe by the life and death of stars are governed at this early time in creation by the repeatable laws of physics and caused in part by the four forces. Thus, the creation of stars and galaxies is a repeating process, not an undetermined random progression of change by the physical laws that have no volition.

Flat Universe, 10^{-36}

At one time, all of humankind believed, based on what they seemed to observe with their own eyes, that Earth was flat. Contrary to popular belief, the Bible does not proclaim that Earth is flat; however, it did declare that the universe was flat long before geometry was discovered. This concept was expressed in the Bible via the metaphor of a tent, which is similar to the metaphors used today to describe the flatness of the universe. Its simplicity belies some astonishing revelations.

The Creator declares the universe is flat, as reflected in the metaphor of a tent spread out to be erected. This flatness is not literally flat like a sheet of paper. A universe with a flat geometry has an actual mass/energy density of space that equals the critical density of gravity. This value is so precise that scientists describe it as resting on a knife's edge between what is called a closed or open universe. For the universe to be geometrically flat now, the density of space-time at a fraction of a second after the Big Bang must have been fine tuned to the critical value to one part in 10^{-60}. It is astonishing that this biblical metaphor describes four different aspects pertaining to this creation and current condition of the universe.

Increased genera follow all ten mass extinctions

> It is he that sitteth upon the circle of Earth, and the inhabitants thereof are as grasshoppers; that stretcheth out the heavens as a curtain, and *spreadeth them out as a tent to dwell in*. (Isaiah 40:22)

Tent metaphor number one: The first facet of this multifaceted metaphor of a tent is yet another reference the Bible makes to the fabric of space. To convey a better understanding of what space is, science also uses fabric as a metaphor. It is space that was spread out exponentially along with mass in the early universe from a state of the lowest possible entropy that ever existed. The speed of this early expansion is calculated by scientists to be faster than the speed of light. Energy/mass contained within space during this initial expansion could not pass *through* space faster than the speed of light, so it must have been the fabric of space itself that was stretched faster than the speed of light while the energy/mass expanded with it.

Tent metaphor number two: The second facet of the metaphor represents the first step in the process being described. The first step in erecting a tent is to spread the tent flat on the ground. This is parallel to the beginning process of creating the universe. Scientists believe that everything we see in the structure of the universe was determined at the earliest point of the first second of the universe's existence. The flatness of the universe was established at that extremely early time in creation. That flatness had to be established at the beginning of creation, just as the laying out of the tent is the first step in its erection, as shown below.

Flat tent image

According to scientists, space-time at creation had to start in an extremely flat state, corresponding with extremely low entropy. It was a difficult and delicate balance at the moment of the creation of energy, matter, and space to achieve these extreme initial conditions. The evidence of the universe's initial order affirms this was not a bang or an explosion, as we generally understand an explosion to be, because neither can produce an isotropic, homogeneous, and flat universe. Creation was an extremely hot, violent, almost instantaneous creation event of energy that expanded and converted in part to mass. It was a creative process, not a destructive process like a bomb, and it started with the fine-tuned balance for a geometrically flat universe.

Tent metaphor number three: The third facet is the spreading of the tent reflecting the distribution of the fabric of space-time. The Standard Model predicts the initial density was fine-tuned to an accuracy of about one part in 10^{-60} for the initial density to agree with the critical density. Critical density refers to the average amount of matter necessary to cause the expansion of the universe to halt, after a period of time. When the actual density of matter equals the critical density, the universe is determined to be geometrically flat. The omega symbol (Ω) is used to represent this geometry. When omega equals one ($\Omega=1$) the geometry is flat, as shown in the picture below. If the actual density is greater than one ($\Omega \geq 1$), the geometry is considered to be closed like the sphere and will collapse back into a crunch. And if the actual density is less than one ($\Omega \leq 1$), the geometry is considered open like a saddle and the universe will expand too fast for proper formation of the universe we see today.

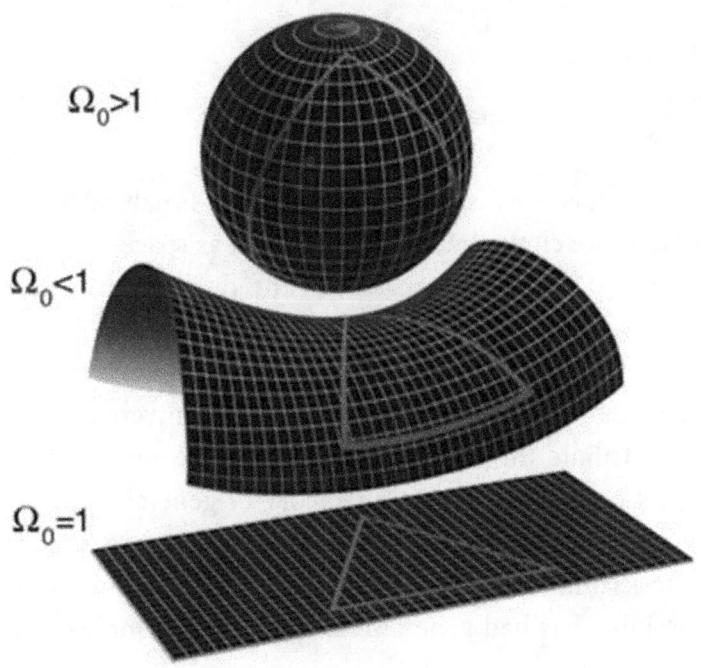

NASA/WMAP Science Team

The combination of the fabric aspect with the distribution aspect of the tent metaphor reveals one of the most famous phenomena in physics. The tent fabric represents the curvature of space, while the tent spreading represents the distribution of space. Theoretical physicist John Archibald Wheeler simplified Einstein's general relativity equation by explaining its two sides: "Space-time tells matter how to move; matter tells space-time how to curve." The equation can *also* be explained using two creation-referencing scriptures of the fabric of space from the Bible.

Curvature of space = Distribution of energy/mass

$$G_{\mu\nu} = -\frac{8\pi G}{c^4} T_{\mu\nu}$$

Isaiah 50:3a = Isaiah 40:22b

On the curvature side of the equation, Isaiah 50:3a declares the heavens are clothed with blackness just as space-time is curved around every object with mass. On the distribution side, Isaiah 40:22b declares the heavens are spread out as a tent in which to dwell, reflecting the distribution of mass/energy at the critical density to produce a flat space-time. To produce a flat universe, the Creator had to distribute the energy/mass precisely to match the critical density as outlined in Einstein's theory of general relativity. This theory has now endured more than one hundred years of intense scientific scrutiny and experimentation. Who would have thought that the Bible has had general relativity covered for thousands of years?

The proclamation of a flat universe is an incredible claim and has been backed by the testing of general relativity through precise instrumentation and cosmological observations. That the

Bible posited it as the first step in creation without sophisticated instruments or advanced math is even more astounding.

This is not a "God of the gaps" proclamation, where God is inserted into an unknown. I am pointing out the knowledge required merely to make the claim of this phenomenon. If or when this phenomenon is understood completely, this will still be an astounding condition of the universe predicted by the author of the Bible and verified thousands of years later through scientific observation.

God declared the universe flat five hundred years before the Greek mathematician Euclid introduced the world to geometry. This is additional proof that God created the laws of physics and mathematics, calling the universe flat before the term "flat" was coined or understood. Living in a three-dimensional world with three-dimensional objects all around us, the concept of a flat universe sounds absurd. But this flatness is not literally flat like the NASA image on the above page, or the flat tent reference of the Bible. Scientists have determined its flatness based on precise measurements by NASA's COBE and WMAP missions, along with ESA's Planck mission.

Tent metaphor number four: A tent spread out on the ground is never perfectly flat. It is impossible to lie out a tent on any surface without the tent having dimples and bumps. Even the heavy gauge of the fabric will cause dimples, creases, and other imperfections. In the same way, God did not use the metaphor of a pristine, glassy lake to describe the universe's flatness. Declaring the universe to be flat (perfect density ratio), the Creator also implies its smooth or homogenous distribution. The dimples and bumps in the tent's fabric is another facet of this metaphor because it reflects the imperfections observed in the CMB, which has temperature variations throughout. These were first affirmed by data from NASA's COBE satellite research program in 1992. These variations actually show both the smoothness and fluctuations of the early universe. Making more precise measurements of the CMB, the WMAP satellite research program identified temperature variations across the universe of only .0002 degrees Kelvin between the hot regions and the cold regions. The dimples in the fabric of the tent represent the fluctuations in the fabric of space-time evident in the CMB.

> These cosmic microwave temperature fluctuations are believed to trace fluctuations in the density of matter in the early universe, as they were imprinted shortly after the Big Bang. This being the case, they reveal a great deal about the early universe and *the origin of galaxies and large scale structure* in the universe.[5]

According to scientists, these minuscule variations at the beginning of creation allowed dark matter, through gravity, to allow normal matter to carry out the creation processes throughout the universe. This is reflected in the formation of the stars, galaxies, and galaxy clusters we observe today. It also underscores the importance of representing this action metaphorically as the first part of the process of "laying out the tent to dwell in," which is the first part of the creation process.

This multi-faceted metaphor of a flat universe implies that God supplied this first-hand knowledge to the scribe who recorded it. To have lain out the initial density of space-time to be flat to a level of one part in 10^{60} or less implies God is the fine tuner of the flatness of the universe.

---

[5] NASA, "WMAP: Wilkinson Microwave Anisotropy Probe," *wmap.gsfc.nasa.gov*

Inflation, 10^{-36}

The Bible also strongly proclaims that the universe is expanding. Five different scribes in twelve scriptures described the expansion of the heavens. Of those twelve, six are written in the past tense, implying a completed task, and six are written in the present tense, implying continual action. This seems to be a contradiction about the same phenomenon.

The universe has been expanding nonstop since the very instance of creation or the Big Bang. However, the Bible references a completed expansion in Jeremiah 10:12 and 51:15, and in Isaiah 51:13, 48:13, and 45:12. The verse that most strongly asserts the idea of expansion was completed at the time of creation is Isaiah 42:5. The word "created" in this verse is translated from the Hebrew word *bara*, which primarily means "a new creation from nothing."

> Thus saith God the Lord, he that created the heavens, and stretched them out. (Isaiah 42:5a)

The scripture declares the heavens were created (*bara*) and space-time was subsequently expanded. The past tense use of the verbs "created" and "expanded" implies a completed task.

In the quest to understand *how* the creation process took place, scientists have developed the Standard Model for the creation of the universe that we can observe. There are two major concerns scientists have with the model: one is called the horizon problem, and the other is the flatness problem. The theory that has been postulated to solve these problems is called inflation, proposed by Alan Guth of MIT.

Inflation is the rapid, exponential expansion of space-time for a fraction of a second during the first second of creation. Scientists believe this action accounts for the uniform temperature of CMB radiation and flatness of space-time. An inflationary period also explains why the universe is homogeneous and isotropic, which implies the characteristics and distribution of space-time were set (created) before inflation began. One of the strongest aspects of the inflation theory is that the rapid exponential expansion ceased, and reverted to expand at a reduced rate. The biblical declarations of a completed expansion and a continual expansion would mirror a model of the inflation theory. Inflation is not a proven scientific phenomenon; however, scientists have embarked on the difficult task of detecting gravitational waves in space, along with other experiments as evidence that inflation actually took place.

Even if scientists are not able to conclude this extremely early phenomenon took place, the Bible's declaration of a completed expansion, and an expansion that continues as observed today, will not change. It is plausible that the use of the past tense of expansion refers to inflation.

Higgs Field, 10^{-12}

The Higgs boson, also known as the "God Particle" is one of the most significant scientific discoveries being one of the fundamental components of the fabric of the universe. While the famous God Particle nickname has garnered publicity, it reflects the importance it plays in the existence of matter. While the extremely short-lived boson was the target of the search, its discovery indicates the presence of an energy field that permeates all of space. That invisible field is appropriately called the Higgs field, which confers mass to particles as they interact with the field. The Higgs field is:

> "the stuff that gives all other particles a mass. Every particle in our universe 'swims' through this Higgs field. Through this interaction every particle gets its mass. Different particles interact with the Higgs field with different strengths,

hence some particles are heavier (have a larger mass) than others...The Higgs field is not considered a force. It cannot accelerate particles, it doesn't transfer energy. However, it interacts universally with all particles (except the massless ones), providing their masses."[6]

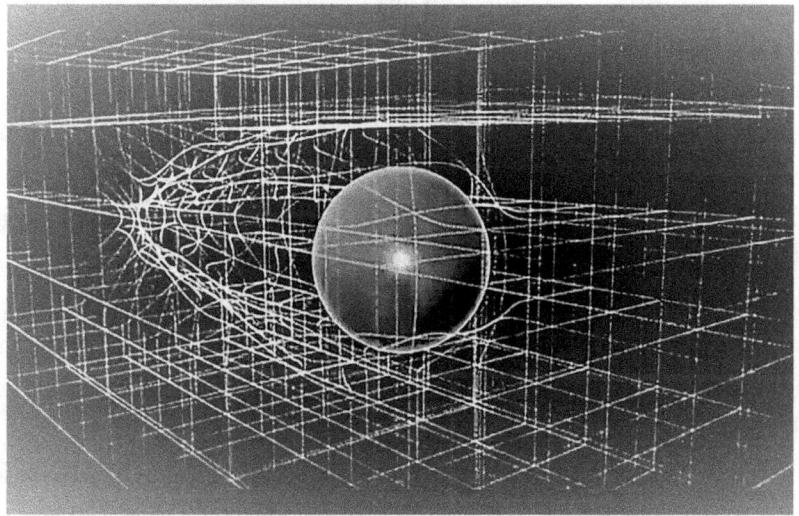

Illustration of a particle in simulated Higgs field

I clothe the heavens with blackness, and *I make sackcloth their covering.* (Isaiah 50:3)

The sackcloth referred to in Isaiah is a perfect analogy of this mysterious cosmological concept. A three-dimensional application of the sackcloth would resemble the Higgs field of the illustration above, which is an artist's representation. The space between the up/down and side-by-side sackcloth mesh allows some massless particles to pass without being hampered, permitting them to travel

---

6   Kurt Riesselmann, "Higgs Boson," *www.fnal.gov*

at the speed of light. Other particles, like the one shown making contact with the mesh (fibers) in the illustration, are slowed, and are considered mass.

For a long time this hypothesis was one of the great mysteries of theoretical physics, but after decades of work by thousands of scientists around the world, it was finally confirmed in 2012 by the largest, most advanced experimental equipment known to humankind. Scientists at the Large Hadron Collider at CERN announced the discovery of the predicted Higgs boson, which provides proof of the Higgs field. Dr. Peter Higgs and François Englert received the Nobel Prize in physics for their work in particle physics after laying the foundation of how this field/particle contributes to the mass of elementary particles. The Creator indeed both clothed the heavens with the fabric of space and covered the heavens with the Higgs field within the greatest second of creation, the first second.

The context of the verse in Isaiah is the heavens or the universe. The first metaphor, of blackness, is a reference to clothing everything with space and was addressed earlier. The second metaphor in this verse is the additional action of covering everything with a fabric like sackcloth. This covering reference to the fabric of space is quite different from the clothing of space itself. To clothe something is to place the fabric on that which is clothed, just as the clothing we wear fits the contours of our body. However, to cover is different than to clothe, in that what covers does not need to continually contour and/or touch that which is covered. The Higgs field permeating space is analogous to air covering the clothed humans on Earth, the air representing the Higgs field.

Space contains fields like the electromagnetic, electron, and many other fields that are generated by field carriers. However, the Higgs field is different in that it needs no carrier; it permeates all of space all the time. The Higgs cannot be removed or turned off; just as the Bible implies, the heavens (all matter) have a covering. The

Increased genera follow all ten mass extinctions

Higgs particle has been often referred to as the "God particle," but it is the field that should be called the "God field," in part because it has a characteristic of the Almighty, in that both are omnipresent.

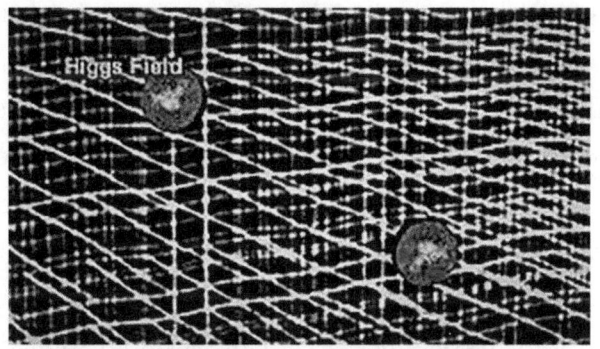

Modern illustration of the Higgs field

Biblical illustration of the Higgs field

The comparison of the modern, scientific illustration with the sackcloth of the Bible shown above is quite striking! One predominant characteristic of the sackcloth is its porous fabric. Stretching the fabric gives it a different density. This fabric is called burlap today and can have holes as big as a quarter inch. In ancient history, this mesh cloth sack was made of a coarsely woven goat hair and was used to carry produce, nuts, and corn. Sackcloth was ideal for grain and other agricultural products because of its high breathability. However, its porous nature meant it could not contain substances smaller than the size of the fabric's weave.

A three-dimensional perspective of sackcloth applied to three-dimensional space would have two major properties. One property would be to slow small objects that move down by resistance, and the other property would be to allow smaller objects to pass through readily. As a metaphor, this loosely woven sackcloth fabric has characteristics similar to the Higgs field that permeates all of space. The Higgs field is a matter field, one of the two fundamental types of fields that make up the universe. The other type of field is a force field like the magnetic force field of Earth, which will be discussed later in the chapter on the creation of the foundations of the Earth.

Mass is the resistance an object offers to having its speed changed. You take a baseball. When you throw it, your arm feels resistance. A shot-put, you feel that resistance. The same way for particles. Where does the resistance come from? And the theory was put forward that perhaps space was filled with an invisible "stuff," an invisible molasses-like "stuff," and when the particles try to move through the molasses, they feel a resistance, a stickiness. It's that stickiness which is where their mass comes from . . . That creates the mass.[7]

Scientists theorize the Higgs field inhibits some elementary particles that interact with the field, obtaining what is considered mass due to "drag" and/or constantly bumping into the field. A second property of the Higgs field allows certain massless elementary particles to pass through the field up to the speed of light. A third property is that it moves like the fabric of space in which it permeates. Again, it is difficult to portray the three-dimensional concept of the Higgs field with any two-dimensional object, but the sackcloth metaphor the Creator used is an excellent analogy to the Higgs field. Everything in the universe is covered by the fabric of this field, just as a fish is covered by all the water it inhabits.

Most references to sackcloth in the Bible describe a garment worn to convey grief, but this is an exception. The sackcloth mentioned in this scripture is really describing space in the universe—it relates to the heavens and makes no reference to sackcloth as funereal garb. Then, and now, sackcloth was the best way of illustrating the characteristics of space and the Higgs field in particular.

Elementary Particles, 10-12

> Through faith we understand that the worlds were framed by the word of God, *so that things which are seen were not made of things which do appear.* (Hebrews 11:3)

---

[7] PBS, *The Charlie Rose Show*, "Brian Greene and Michael Tuts on Higgs Boson.", July 8, 2012.

In about AD 60, the God of the Bible predicted that everything physical (seen) was made of things that *cannot* be seen. A key word in this verse is "made," translated from the Greek word *ginomai*, which could mean either "to become" or "be made." This can refer to the very beginning of creation, similar to the Hebrew word *bara* used in Genesis 1:1 because subatomic particles were created very early in creation. The things we see today (mass) are made of subatomic particles like quarks and leptons, which simply cannot be seen. In the original language, the latter part of this scripture is written in the present tense. This prediction by the Creator is a reference to elementary particles. Atoms do not fit the description of the unseen things because we can see them today through powerful microscopes.

In addition, not everything is made of atoms. One example is one of the most abundant forms of matter in the universe: plasma. Of course, we can see the sun and the stars of the universe, along with the Northern Lights, also called aurora borealis, all of which are made of plasma. This is yet another prediction by the Creator that empirical evidence has substantiated. God also said these things *were* made, past tense, which is also correct because it is confirmed by his own law of conservation of mass/energy that once made, it cannot be destroyed.

Elementary particles are theorized to have been created within the first second and constitute the framework of all matter (things that are seen). Even the largest, most advanced detector, the Large Hadron Collider at CERN, cannot see an elementary particle. It can only detect the presence of such particles after a proton collision has occurred. This is a seventeen-mile ring of superconducting magnets with a number of accelerating structures to boost the speed of the particles to near the speed of light to collide them and record the collision.

Up to the time of the discovery of elementary particles, the biblical statement in Hebrews 11:3—"things which are seen were not made of things which do appear"—seemed like a classic oxymoron. From the discovery of the electron of an atom to the zoo of subatomic particles known today, now we know that elementary particles are invisible, just as the Bible predicts.

Initial Conditions, $10^{-43} \sim 10^{-12}$

> In order to produce a universe resembling the one in which we live, the Creator would have to aim for an absurdly tiny volume of the phase space of possible universes—about $1/10^{10(123)}$ of the entire volume, for the situation under consideration.[8]

The situation under consideration is the extraordinarily low entropy and necessary conditions at creation. However, according to the aforementioned biblical claims of the first second of creation and their compatibility with scientific observations, the fine-tuner of the initial conditions of creation is the God of the Bible. Roger Penrose, a famous British physicist, actually figured the probability of these initial conditions. The above quotation is his conclusion, an actual calculation of the possibility of a "Creator" hitting the target necessary to the initial conditions of the universe at creation. Penrose's calculation is the odds against the Creator's ability to accomplish such a feat. The Creator of the Bible predicted the phenomena of the first second of creation outlined in this chapter. How can the antiquated book called the Bible accurately describe what took place at the beginning of creation without it being firsthand knowledge? In other words, God himself was there and created the phenomena as claimed.

---

[8] Roger Penrose, *The Emperor's New Mind*. (Oxford: Oxford University Press, 1989), 444.

The number $1/10^{10(123)}$ makes the astronomical number called a googol (10^{100}) look small. As a matter of fact, it is larger than a googolplex ($10^{10(100)}$). Those are the odds against the Creator as a single entity accomplishing the feat. Not only did the Creator reveal the initial conditions of the universe, he did it through five different scribes over a period of fifteen hundred years, which informs us this is a divine revelation.

The components of life and the origin of death (entropy) of the universe began within the initial conditions of the universe and not nine billion years later on Earth. The fundamentals of life are found in the first second of creation, not in amino acids (which are essential for life, and which came much later). The concept of death is built in the finite amount of energy released at creation, along with the first and second laws of thermodynamics in the first second of creation, not when Adam sinned. The blueprints of everything, including life and death, are established within the first second of creation. This is the essence of Genesis 1:1: "In the beginning, God created the heavens and the Earth."

That first second is prodigiously fascinating; inferring God is the fine-tuner of the universe. Before we move on to the remaining 13.8 billion years of creation, I will compare the events of this first second to a snapshot taken one second from the start of a human foot race. The purpose is to use this information to infer what happened before the creation event.

Cosmogony—Before the Beginning

Before the starting line of time for the universe is a period called cosmogony. Cosmogony refers to the origin of the universe, before "time = 0," i.e., before the Big Bang. Cosmology, in contrast, refers to how the universe operates after the beginning. The Bible speaks about activities that occurred before the start of time itself. Cosmogony is being addressed after the first second because there

Increased genera follow all ten mass extinctions

is no physical reference to analyze what happened "before time." It is necessary to look through the earliest part of the first second to ascertain any understanding of what occurred before time. Imagine attending the summer Olympic Games to see the world's fastest runners compete for the gold. Before reaching this elite stage, the participants would have had to qualify in many races in other venues just to have the privilege of entering the games. Once qualified, the athletes would be required to race in heats to shrink the field to the fastest of the fast.

In the final race of the competition, the runners crouch in their pre-race position, fingers mere centimeters behind the perfectly straight starting line painted on the track. Between the starting line and the finish line lie one hundred meters, a gold medal, and the prospect of athletic glory. As the race official raises the starter's pistol, the audience holds their collective breath, and the racers tense as everyone listens for the bang.

Bang! One second into the race, a picture is taken. Although this picture is of the race itself (at the very beginning), it contains information of activities that took place before the race. The picture shows runners in the process of releasing from the starting blocks with their muscles flexing and faces grimacing. We see athletes with lean muscular bodies, which indicates there was training before the start of the race. It also shows the athletes in sporting attire that is suitable for running, not snow skiing, implying knowledge and preparation for a particular race. All the runners started at the same time, signifying they had prior knowledge of the purpose of the start signal. By examining that picture, we can determine general activities that took place *before* the bang of the starter's pistol.

Similarly, we can glean information about what occurred before the start of creation. The information is embodied in the extreme order across the spectrum of initial phenomena. The one-second picture shows the greatest oxymoron of all times: an explosion of order.

To ascertain what has taken place in the universe back to the first fraction of a second after creation requires information to fuel the equations of the laws of physics. Furthermore, the equations themselves are information. Any and all equations are dead without injecting information for them to work. From time = 0 to 10^{-43} [9] of the first second, there was no time for the evolution of information, yet it was inherent in both quantum mechanics and general relativity activity. Judging by the inherent information in the first second after creation, the Bible is correct in declaring that wisdom and, by inference, information existed before creation.

According to the Bible, information and God's plan crossed the creation event from before the foundation of the world (time) into creation and is manifested in the extreme first part of the first second. The scriptures below characterize wisdom as being with the Creator before creation (Big Bang). The pure organization of the galactic events of the first second implies a plan before beginning, from everlasting.

---

9   Planck time, the time it takes a photon to travel a Planck length (1.6×10^{-35}), the smallest measure of time that has any meaning.

Increased genera follow all ten mass extinctions

The LORD possessed me in the beginning of his way, before his works of old. I was set up from everlasting, from the beginning, or ever Earth was. When there were no depths, I was brought forth; when there were no fountains abounding with water. Before the mountains were settled, before the hills was I brought forth: While as yet he had not made Earth, nor the fields, nor the highest part of the dust of the world. When he prepared the heavens, I was there: when he set a compass upon the face of the depth: (Proverbs 8:22–27)

Another indicator of our one-second creation picture is the lowest state of entropy or the highest order the universe has ever experienced. That means it was created that way, containing all the properties that exist, in the first second of creation. No chaos, no explosion; a release of energy. Within extremely tiny fragments of the first second, the universe started with the greatest order possible; there was literally no time for evolution, guided or unguided. The picture indicates it was created that way from a plan on the other side of time.

This order is made manifest in another actual picture of the cosmos, the CMB radiation. This is not a snapshot of the first second after creation; it is the afterglow of the original release of energy at creation, which manifested itself an estimated 380,000 years after. Today, it still contains a wealth of information about creation.

The term Big Bang is something of a misnomer, and it masks the smoothness and orderliness of the CMB (shown below).

NASA Image of cosmic microwave background radiation (CMB)

This relates to the smoothness of the release of energy at creation. This image represents the entire universe. The darker spots are the cold areas and the lighter spots are the warmer areas. However, the difference between these two extremes is only one hundred thousandth of a degree centigrade. No explosion can produce anything near this smoothness across the entire detectable universe.

The first second has been often referred to as the blueprint of the universe. But this one-second description or snapshot reveals the establishment of the structure of the universe. That's like declaring a framed house or skyscraper's completed steel framing is the blueprint of the structure. The image of the framing of the house and skyscraper implies the existence of a plan. The blueprint had to come *before* the framing. That blueprint for creation is the origin of the universe from the Creator before the beginning of time.

Chapter 3

Between Genesis 1:1 & 1:2

What happened between Genesis 1:1 and 1:2? This is often referred to as the great gap in the creation account. Now we go from the first second of creation, Genesis 1:1, and proceed to the formation of our solar system, Genesis 1:2. Based upon Earth's estimated age of 4.5 billion years, there are about nine billion years from the first second of creation to the formation of our solar system, which contains Earth. Let's start with the elements of which everything is made.

Simple Elements

According to the Standard Model of cosmology, it is estimated that within the first few minutes after creation, the simple elements were created: hydrogen, helium, and small amounts of lithium. After the creation of the laws of physics and elementary particles, the base material and means by which the universe would be formed were established. A process called Big Bang nucleosynthesis occurred during the initial extreme heat, when the low mass elements hydrogen and helium, and a smaller amount of lithium, were formed. Lithium, with its three protons, demonstrates complexity through the complete establishment of quantum mechanics; quantum electrodynamics, wave-particle duality, quantum optics, the uncertainty principle, and all that was discovered later about the subatomic world. At this early stage of creation, the chemical laws were *established*; they did not *evolve* over time. The remaining elements were produced by the same established process of fusion.

Later in time, through stellar nucleosynthesis, when the conditions were produced within the life and death of the stars, more complex elements were made. The heat and pressure of fusion are the process by which every element of the periodic table is formed. Elements heavier than iron are formed through the supernova death of stars. Hydrogen, the most abundant element in the universe, is the primary form of stellar fuel. Hydrogen and helium still make up an estimated 98 percent of the ordinary matter of the universe. The remaining elements created in stars represent just 2 percent. Just as a crude oil refinery uses different levels of heat to extract gasoline, propane, butane, and alcohol from the oil, various levels of heat and pressure in stars inversely produce the different elements.

In addition to the elements within the life and death process of stars, many other phenomena were brought forth, such as novae, supernovae, black holes, dwarf stars, neutron stars, pulsars, magnetars, accretion disks, and quasars. All of these star "products" are produced by the laws of physics. Gasoline does not evolve from crude oil; it's created through a process. Just as the growth of a tree produces more of the same, the growth of the universe produces more of the same, not an evolution in diversity. For the next 13.8 billion years, the universe grew in quantity of stars, planets, and galaxies by the established processes and through the generations of the stars to what we see today, so where is the cosmic evolution of improving complexity? The changes are limited to quantity and scope according to processes that were fixed from the beginning.

Dark Matter—Creator's Dust

One of the greatest mysteries of physics and cosmology today is dark matter. The sheer amount of matter in the massive universe is mind-boggling, and to our astonishment, only the baryonic matter, representing 5 percent of the total composition, can be seen.

The advent of the telescope opened the night sky for Galileo some four hundred years ago, and countless other scientists have used this invention to garner knowledge of the cosmos. The technical advancements of visible light telescopes and the array of telescopes covering the entire spectrum of light and sound have enhanced that search. Computer-controlled ground and space-based observatory systems with unparalleled accuracy have probed the sky relentlessly for the elusive 80 percent of all matter in the universe. This enormous amount of matter is not made of atoms, yet it contains mass and is totally invisible, hence its name, dark matter.

According to the Standard Model of the universe, dark matter is the scaffolding or structure of the galactic universe. It is called dark because it cannot be detected directly, and little is known about it. The European Space Agency's (ESA) Planck Project, utilizing the latest advanced technology, estimates dark matter represents approximately 80 percent of all the matter in the universe and 26.8 percent of the total composition of the universe.

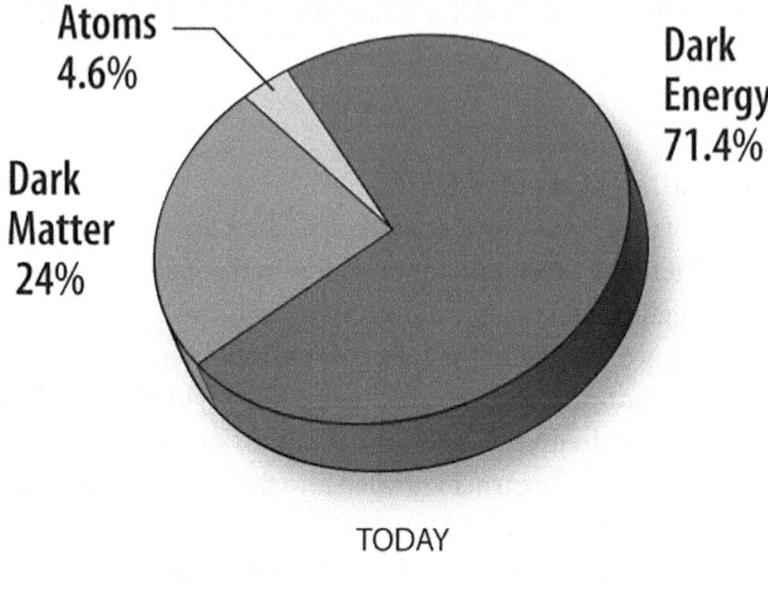

TODAY

NASA Image

Scientists contend the amount of visible matter does not provide enough gravity to account for the orbital speed of stars within galaxies. They conclude that more matter must be present to exert the gravity required to keep stars orbiting at high speeds without flying apart from the galaxy.

Then called "missing mass," dark matter was first theorized by Jan Oort and Fritz Zwicky in the 1930s to account for the source of gravity beyond what that of the ordinary visible matter. Later, Vera Rubin and her colleagues affirmed the theory by the gravitational relationship between dark matter and the rotational speed of stars within galaxies.

Did the Creator leave any clues about this enormous component of the universe? The mysteries of science have been extracted from nature at a high price, owing to the time and labor of thousands of scientists over several centuries. This knowledge is not found on the surface; it must be relentlessly sought, even against the toughest odds. In the same vein, the predictions made by the Creator are not on the surface and certainly are not conveniently enumerated in a sequential or chronological order in the Bible. These metaphors are peppered throughout, hidden until their revelation is possible.

Scientists theorize that dark matter is a particle, but are unsure of what it really is and how it functions. The eventual understanding of dark matter will not change the fact that the Bible described this phenomenon long ago.

> The LORD possessed me in the beginning of his way, before his works of old. I was set up from everlasting, from the beginning, or ever Earth was. When there were no depths, I was brought forth; when there were no fountains abounding with water. Before the mountains were settled, before the hills was I brought forth: While as yet he had not made Earth, nor the fields, nor the *highest part of the dust of the world*. (Proverbs 8:22–26)

It is improbable that an Iron Age human (scribe) could declare there is dust beyond Earth. It is yet more improbable to describe the same dust as being superior or the highest dust of the world (expanse). The Bible declared there is dust in space, and this particular dust, of all the stellar dust, is of the highest order. There is no higher order and characteristic than that of the invisible "dust" of outer space, which scientists call dark matter. This is not normal baryonic matter of which we are made. Its importance in the physical structure of the universe is of the utmost: it is vital to maintaining critical density for proper expansion and operation of the universe itself.

When the Creator reveals aspects of his creation that have not been discovered and/or fully understood, our interpretation is limited to what we know. Over time, as we achieve greater knowledge, we perfect or refine our interpretation of these metaphors. This is not a change in the Bible but an increase in our understanding of the application of this and other metaphors. Jesus's disciples refined their understanding of him and his teachings only after his death when they realized that Jesus came at that time to be a sacrifice and not the promised king. They changed when this increased knowledge gave them a better understanding, and they began to proclaim that Jesus would return to be that king. Thank God, they were not too narrow-minded to adjust their understanding of God's will and purpose.

In Proverbs 8:22-26, the depths, fountains with water, mountains, and hills are described alongside a reference to Earth. However, in the last sentence, the dust is a separate reference that is part of the world, not the Earth. "The world" is also a reference to a greater area than Earth.

Two commentaries from two nineteenth century theologians demonstrate that this is not a new concept brought about by the discovery of dark matter. Theologians Adam Clarke and Daniel Whedon each put forth a bold and progressive interpretation of Proverbs 8:26. They compared the dust to the likes of atomic and subatomic particles and not to dust on Earth.

> The highest part of the dust of the world - תורפע שאר לבת rosh aphroth tebel, "*the first particle of matter.*" The prima material, the primitive atom. All these verses (verses 3-29) are a periphrasis for I existed before creation, consequently before time was. I dwelt in God as a principle which might be communicated in its influences to intellectual beings when formed.[10]

---

10   *Bible Hub*, "Proverbs 8," www.biblehub.com

Nor the highest part of the dust of the world — תורפע שאר לבת, (rosh "haphroth tebhel,) <u>the first dust of the world</u> — the primeval atoms, seemingly opposed to the hhutsoth — the observable part. "World," (tebhel,) a poetic word from ללב, (balal,) one of the meanings of which is to mix, mingle—the compounded mass of Earth. The sense of the whole, throwing off the poetic garb, and carrying forward the verb from the preceding verse, appears to be: *I was produced while yet he had not made the land,* neither the observable exterior nor the interior atoms of the complex globe. Some expositors fancy that the highest part of the dust of Earth means man himself, originally formed of the dust of Earth. The drift of the thought in Proverbs 8:23-27, is seemingly this: We have, first, the proposition, (Proverbs 8:23,) I existed before Earth (as a whole) existed. This is amplified in sundry particulars, first, (Proverbs 8:24,) before the fluid parts, the oceans and streams; second, (Proverbs 8:25,) before the solid parts, especially the more prominent and observable, as the mountains and hills; third, (ver. 26,) an amplification of this again, descending to other particulars—the surface of the land and its internal components—*the original atoms or particles* of the same. Wisdom was before all these.[11]

These scriptures are a definite reference to the earliest stages of creation, the first dust of the world. It turns out to be just as Clarke stated. If not the first, then one of the first particles of creation, the highest part of matter is dark matter. The Creator speaks of possessing wisdom to create the universe before the creation event. Clarke and Whedon referred to this dust as the primeval atoms, the first dust of the world. Whedon points out this highest dust opposed

---

11   Daniel Whedon, *Commentary on the Old Testament–Volume 6*

characteristics to the observable part, making it invisible. These theologians, not scientists, demonstrated that revelations from God to humankind occurred long after the canon of scripture. The Bible made this proclamation around 1000 BC. Outside of divine knowledge, how could any terrestrial creature have known about the dusts of the cosmos?

By his spirit he hath garnished the heavens. (Job 26:13a)

Here in Job 26:13, the Creator garnished (beautified) the heavens by way of his spirit. The word "spirit" is the Hebrew word *ruwach*, which is translated into various English words in the Bible, such as "spirit, wind, and breath." In addition to these translations, the most significant translation represents the Spirit of God when the word is capitalized. To translate this scripture, most translations use the words "wind" or "breath," both of which are an invisible force. By the invisible nature of dark matter's characteristics, it seems logical that the invisible force used by God would be, in fact, dark matter. The wind metaphor relates to that which is affected by the wind by way of its physical influence, similar to dark matter when it encounters ordinary matter. However, it is not a reference to solar winds, which are plasma outbursts from the sun or a star. The heavens are indeed garnished by the distribution of the invisible dark matter of the universe.

The most magnificently designed architectural works in the world use various construction and aesthetic methods to hide the framing that supports their structure. Likewise, dark matter is the invisible framework of the universe that supports the formation of stars, galaxies, and baryonic matter and their arrangement in the universe. The Creator is also the architect of the universe, and he is intent on showing off the greatness of his work. The Creator used invisible dark matter to hide the framework and allow full view of the glorious night sky both far and near.

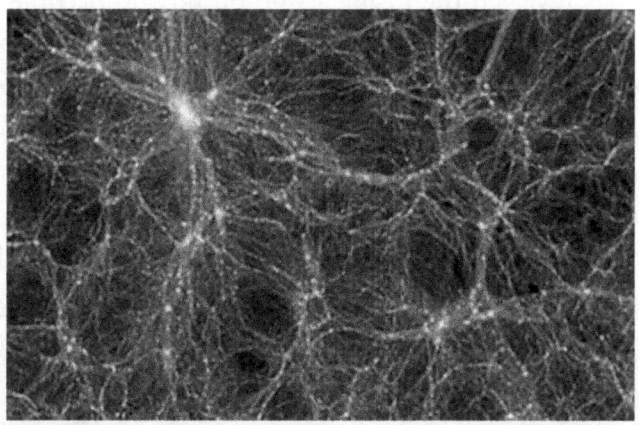

NASA Image. The cosmic web showing galaxies and galaxy clusters coalescing along invisible dark matter.

The use of a visible framework, such as ordinary matter, would be unacceptable because it would prevent his handiwork from being displayed; the heavens would look like a near cloud, obscuring the beauty of many of the stars, galaxies, and the remaining cosmos. The Hubble telescope would have had a much smaller impact on our knowledge, and many of the magnificent pictures it has taken would not exist. The universe would be hidden in a cloud of cosmic dust. That would be tragic.

Stars

> In them hath he set a tabernacle for the sun, which is as a bridegroom coming out of his chamber, and rejoiceth as a strong man to run a race. (Psalm 19:4b–5)

The beauty of the cosmos is found in the stars. We use the stars as a metaphor for a person who shines above all others. The Creator has revealed the inside scoop on how to become a literal star to King David in the Book of Psalms, some three millennia ago. The bridegroom chamber mentioned in the above passage is a metaphor for a secret (hidden) place where the seed of life comes together, driven by the attraction of a man and a woman in the consummation of marriage. Likewise, the birth of stars occurs in the hidden clouds of a nebula where the seeds of stars in the form of dust come together, driven by gravity and electromagnetism, to begin the life of a star. The nebula is the chamber where this hidden union takes place. We cannot see this phenomenon without infrared and X-ray telescopes piercing the dust. This process affirms the Creator did not create the stars in some "mature" state. The life and death of stars takes millions of years. This biblical revealed duration is not compatible with a literal seven-day creation period.

Like a runner, our newborn sun joins the other stars in a race around a track called a galaxy. The speed at which the stars along the edge of a galaxy travel is just as fast as those nearer the center. Scientists have determined this high speed of orbiting stars of galaxies would be impossible without a massive amount of gravity—which comes from dark matter, as visible matter is not sufficient to meet the gravitational "needs" of these planetary bodies.

Our sun (star) is estimated to orbit around its tabernacle (the Milky Way) at a speed that exceeds five hundred thousand miles per hour. That's certainly a racing speed! Our sun, like any competitive race, is run at the maximum speed possible. The Creator also knew about the dark matter effect of keeping our fast-moving sun orbiting in the outer perimeter of the galaxy. The formation of the stars, and maximum orbital speed alluded to in the Bible, mirrors years of scientific research.

Some point to the relative fast-burning blue stars as evidence of a young Earth. This is a very limited assessment of all stars of the universe. Blue stars, also known as type "O" stars by astronomers, represent less than 1 percent of the billions of stars of the universe. The lives of these blue stars are estimated to be from a few million to over one hundred million years. The relatively cooler stars, type "M," have an estimated life from two hundred million to ten trillion years, and the oldest M type stars represent some 75 percent of all stars in the universe. If we are to consider the age of the stars in the context of the age of creation, we should not ignore the other 99 percent, which are not blue stars. According to the Bible, the formation of stars is a very lengthy process as observed in the various stages of different star systems.

> Canst thou bind the sweet influences of Pleiades, or loose the bands of Orion? (Job 38:31)

God created the process that makes stars and also arranged the constellations. The Creator asked Job a question that was unanswerable by any man at the time while demonstrating his firsthand knowledge of his own works. His total control of the constellations mentioned in this verse is shown first by demonstrating that he can bind the stars together and loose them at his choosing. The open star cluster known as the Pleiades or the Seven Sisters, referred to in the above scripture, is held (bound) together by gravity, as described by God's question to Job. The Bible predicted the Seven Sisters were bound together before Newton discovered the effect of gravity on Earth and in the heavens. Scientific observation has determined indeed that the stars of the Pleiades are held together by gravity. God is rearranging the cosmos to his liking. Constellations can be very deceptive with respect to the actual locations of the stars as they are viewed from our place in the cosmos. Stars that appear to be side by side can in fact be millions of light years apart relative to the observer, negating the effect of gravity.

Unlike the bound star cluster of the Pleiades, the stars that form the belt of Orion are not bound together by gravity, just as the Creator declared. He predicted the stars in Orion's belt were moving apart in a specified direction. The movement of the stars that make up Orion's belt in the Milky Way is called the "proper motion of stars." The biblical idea of moving stars contrasts with humankind's ancient belief that stars were fixed points of light. Indeed, this movement is extremely difficult to detect without high-tech instruments.

The three stars of Orion's belt seem to be in alignment with each other, but this is an illusion because the stars are at different distances from Earth. Orion's belt consists of Alnitak, the eastern star; Alnilam, the middle star; and Mintaka, the western star. This motion is extremely small and can only be detected with high-tech instruments like the Hipparcos star catalog mission launched in 1989 by the European Space Agency.[12]

From the position of Earth in the Milky Way, the three stars of Orion's belt are actually moving apart and not toward each other. The Bible predicted the loosening of Orion's belt. The NASA Astrophysics Data System offers scientific proof of the movement of the Orion Nebula cluster, indicating that it is not a bound system. The following statement is a reference to Orion:

> Although there is a clear concentration in the proper motion diagram, both the remaining dispersion of the internal motions and the distribution of "members" as projected on

---

12   Science@ESA, "Charting the Galaxy: From Hipparcos to Gaia," online video, YouTube, https://www.youtube.com/watch?v=1rK5lq6gPnM

the sky indicate that the stars in this region are not bound as one system, but do have a common origin.[13]

Canst thou bring forth Mazzaroth in his season? or canst thou guide Arcturus with his sons? (Job 38:32)

Here, God's reference to the constellation Mazzaroth deals with the placement of the stars relative to the movement of the Earth. This constellation is located such that it can be seen only at a particular time of year. This corresponds to the relative placement of Earth and our location on it. God speaks of Arcturus as moving, needing to be guided, moving along with smaller stars. First, Arcturus has a high proper motion, which means it is a fast-moving star relative to our solar system and the visual position of Earth. The Bible made this prediction over 3,500 years ago when these fifty-two smaller stars (the sons) could not be seen with the naked eye. For thousands of years, it was presumed to be a single star that shone brightly. Improved technology allowed Quentin Parker of the Australian Astronomical Observatory to discover the stellar stream in 1971. This stellar stream, called the Arcturus Stream, is made up of approximately fifty-two smaller stars that follow the same path. The Creator used the word "guide" to reference a unique path, which stellar observation affirms. Arcturus is not moving with the general stream of stars in the Milky Way. Instead, it takes a path perpendicular to the galactic disk. This stellar stream is theorized to be a remnant of a galaxy that merged with the Milky Way.

Job and every other human to date have enjoyed the Pleiades and Orion. The Creator correctly described the holding together of the Pleiades star cluster. Opposite to this action, the Creator is

---

[13] K.P. Tian, F. van Leeuwen, et al, "Proper motions of stars in the region of the Orion Nebula cluster (C 0532-054)," *Astronomy and Astrophysics Supplement*, v. 118: 503–515.

moving stars apart in his reference to the loosening of Orion's belt. And he moves the stars across the Milky Way in his reference to Arcturus and its then-unknown stream of small stars. It is stunning that the formation and movement of the stars have painted a picture relative to the position of Earth. God is saying he painted the picture with stars as dots for humans on Earth to see. This holds true for every visible constellation. The rhetorical question God asked Job should be asked today to all humankind. Can we or any other entity create or arrange the stars?

> Seek him that maketh the seven stars and Orion, and turneth the shadow of death into the morning and maketh the day dark with night. (Amos 5:8a)

The above verse is another reference to the Creator's control of dark matter to locate stars to his liking and purpose. The use of the words "maketh" and "turneth" in this scripture indicates that the stars are being made continually. Scientists have discovered that the universe is teeming with stars in various stages of development, from birth to death, just as the Bible describes.

Stars actually have a lifecycle. The process of life and death of the stars is necessary for the life of subsequent stars. Amos 5:8 was written in the context of the creation and lifecycle of stars. This poetic metaphor of turning the shadow of death into the morning means to turn death into a new beginning. The death of stars continues to supply seeds for new stars similar to the lifecycle of plants on Earth, since as plants die they become fertilizer for new plant life.

So, the death of one is the new beginning (morning) of another. The cycle continues as life (day) turns to night (death). Within the lifecycle of the stars, all of the elements of the periodic table are made. The stars are the furnaces that produce the elements of the universe, turning the death of stars into new beginnings for the creation of additional stars, planets, moons, comets, and every other component of the universe. The "day" is the illumination of the star, which turns into night as it runs out of fuel, completing the total cycle of the life and death of the stars.

> These are the generations of the heavens and of Earth when they were created, in the day that the LORD God made Earth and the heavens. (Genesis 2:4)

The vast number of stars of the heavens is built upon the generations of other stars. Just as the Earth is declared a part of these generations, so are all the other billions upon billions of planets, rocks, comets, and other heavenly bodies. This process guided by the Creator has yielded the universe we see today.

Galaxies

> As late as the 1920s, astronomers thought all of the stars in the universe were contained inside of the Milky Way. It wasn't until Edwin Hubble discovered a special star known as a Cepheid variable, which allowed him to precisely measure distances, that astronomers realized that the fuzzy patches once classified as nebula were actually separate galaxies.[14]

---

14 Nola Taylor Redd, "Milky Way Galaxy: Facts About Our Galactic Home," *Space.com*, http://www.space.com/19915-milky-way-galaxy.html

What we commonly call a galaxy today was a relatively recent discovery in the early twentieth century by Edwin Hubble and the then-new 100-inch Hooker telescope on Mount Wilson in California. Before the use of telescopes of that size, no one was able to see clearly enough to make accurate determinations about what the nebulous patches were.

And lest thou lift up thine eyes unto heaven, and when thou seest the sun, and the moon, and the stars, even all the host of heaven. (Deuteronomy 4:19)

Thus, the heavens and the Earth were finished, and all the *host* of them. (Genesis 2:1)

The word "host" is used in the Bible to represent a particular group, whether it is an army or group of stars. Deuteronomy 4:19 makes a distinction between the sun, moon, and stars, and then refers to all as the host of heaven. The use of "host" is also plural, referring to the many galaxies of the heavens. The biblical statement that the heavens were filled with actual galaxies was made in 750 BC, at a time when it was believed that all glowing objects in the night sky were stars. This shows again God's foreknowledge of the composition of the cosmos.

Increased genera follow all ten mass extinctions

NASA-Hubble Deep Field

The famous picture (above) taken by the Hubble Space telescope called the Hubble Deep Field is a visualization of the hosts of heaven. What you see in this picture are only galaxies, not stars, since at the distance at which the picture was taken, stars cannot be seen. After the construction of the 100-inch Hooker telescope, more and more advanced telescopes have opened the heavens to humankind's gaze. Now we understand that our own Milky Way galaxy contains an estimated one hundred to four hundred *billion* stars. Galaxies represent most of 5 percent of the ordinary matter in the universe. There are an estimated one hundred to three hundred billion galaxies in the observable universe. God does indeed have star power!

Galaxy Clusters

> ...that stretcheth out the heavens as a curtain, and spreadeth them out as a tent to dwell in. (Isaiah 40:22b)

The earlier metaphor of a tent fabric laid out in preparation for erection demonstrates the galactic layout, including galaxy clusters. As a metaphor, the imperfections of the tent material resemble a computer-generated simulation of the cosmic web of galaxies and galaxy clusters. Scientists theorize that the formation and structure of galaxies and galaxy clusters are evident in the tiny fluctuations of temperature measurements of the CMB.

Bible's tent material image

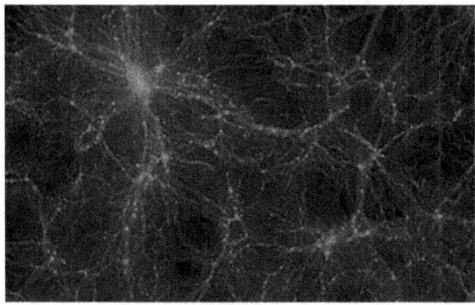

Scientific image

The Creator's description of the layout of the universe is uncanny. Together, the two above pictures are worth a thousand words. The image of the tent material is a facsimile of the image of the galactic structure of the entire universe. The collection of galaxies, constituting the grand scope of the universe, is laid out in the texture of the fabric of tent material.

Expansion of the Universe

One of the major scientific discoveries of the twentieth century was that the universe is expanding. Hubble is credited with this discovery. Without an expanding universe, the materials could not have cooled and formed into the atoms and elements we see today. The CMB radiation is evidence of that cooling process.

As humankind continues to make giant strides in understanding the universe, the Creator has a record of his knowledge of an expanding universe dating back some 2,700 years. He has claimed he is behind the expansion, just as he has claimed he created the universe from *the beginning*. Below are several examples of God speaking through his scribes in the Bible to let the world know who created the universe and who is causing it to expand.

The expanding universe is not the heavenly bodies moving through space away from each other. It is space itself that is stretching, and carrying everything with it. In Psalm 104:2 below, the Bible accurately describes the expansion phenomenon with its metaphor of a curtain, which represents the fabric of space. Like a curtain that is opening, it is space that is expanding. The other verses also listed below speak of a continually expanding universe.

> Who coverest thyself with light as with a garment: *who stretchest out the heavens like a curtain.* (Psalm 104:2)

> Thus saith the Lord, thy redeemer, and he that formed thee from the womb, I am the Lord that maketh all things; that *stretcheth forth the heavens* alone; that spreadeth abroad Earth by myself. (Isaiah 44:24)

> The burden of the word of the Lord for Israel, saith the Lord, which *stretcheth forth the heavens,* and layeth the foundation of Earth, and formeth the spirit of man within him. (Zechariah 12:1)

> Which alone *spreadeth out the heavens,* and treadeth upon the waves of the sea. (Job 9:8)

> He stretcheth out the north over the empty place, and hangeth Earth upon nothing. (Job 26:7)

Earlier, I referenced Isaiah 50:3 where the Creator spoke about clothing everything with blackness (space) and covered all things with sackcloth, which is the Higgs field that permeates all of space. That affirms that space is not "nothing" or "empty." While space is something, this empty place beyond space, which began to expand at a finite time called the Big Bang, does not yet contain anything, including space. However, here in Job 26:7, the Creator speaks of stretching the north (heavens) into the empty place. The phrase "empty place" is from the Hebrew word *tohuw,* which means "vacant" or "empty." The empty place is what existed before creation: emptiness, absolute nothing. From the time of creation, space-time along with all the matter within has been expanding into the empty place just as the Bible declares. This is spoken of in the present tense, indicating a continual extension of space.

One limitation that pops into our head is the first law of thermodynamics, which says matter and energy cannot be created. However, space is not energy, matter, forces, or fields (though it certainly has the ability to contain any and all of these.) If space is not any of these, then it does not violate the first law. It is debatable if space is actually being created or growing as the energy from the initial Big Bang along with dark energy is causing the universe to expand.

Increased genera follow all ten mass extinctions

This is an unknown phenomenon, which is impossible to examine; at this point it can be said that "stretching" and "creating" space-time is effectively the same. However, the Bible declares space is being created continually. If it were necessary to clothe everything with space at creation, from that point on, the continual expansion of the universe would need additional space to expand into. Throughout the 13.8 billion years of expansion, space had to facilitate the growing universe. Since space is not nothing, it requires continual creation to accommodate the expansion.

The later part of Job 26:7 states that the Earth hangs on nothing. The Hebrew word *bĕliymah*, a noun, is translated to "nothing," meaning the Earth is not hanging upon anything tangible. This is the only use of this Hebrew word in the Bible, making it difficult to compare it with other biblical uses of the word. As a matter of fact, it is the theory of general relativity that suggests that the Earth is held in orbit around the sun by the curvature of space. It is not "hanging on" anything.

> I form the light, and create darkness: (Isaiah 45:7a)

In Isaiah 45:7a, the Bible also speaks of a continual creation (*bara*) of the blackness, or darkness, called space. Light is also a continual presence, so the Bible speaks correctly about the nature of light. These phenomena manifest in the present tense as they flow in time from the present into the past and on into the future. Just as he claimed in Isaiah 50:1 to clothe everything with the fabric of space, here he talks of his creation of space, or the darkness we continually see in the heavens.

An Accelerating Universe

Until the discovery of dark energy in the 1990s, scientists were convinced gravity was causing the expansion of the universe to slow. Experimental scientists Adam Riess, Brian Schmidt, and Saul Perlmutter and their teams set out to measure how much gravity was slowing down the universe. In 1998 this research led to one of the biggest surprises in cosmology with their observation that the universe is actually accelerating, which ran opposite to everyone's expectations. The mystery force theorized to cause this acceleration of expansion is referred to as dark energy. How, exactly, the acceleration is powered remains one the most profound mysteries of physics and cosmology. Scientists estimate that dark energy makes up some 73 percent of the universe. Lots of questions tend to flow from the idea of dark energy. Like dark matter, the "dark" in "dark energy" refers to its unknown aspect. The scriptures below are also references to the stretching of the fabric of space by the Creator.

> Who coverest thyself with light as with a garment: who stretchest out the heavens like a curtain. (Psalm 104:2)

> . . . that stretcheth out the heavens as a curtain. (Isaiah 40:22b)

In Psalms 104:2, the Hebrew word *heyry* is translated to curtain, which means "a hanging drape." However, in Isaiah 40:22b, the Hebrew word *doq*, used once in all scripture, means "a thin curtain" or "veil." The solitary use of this word in the Bible reflects its uniqueness to the heavens. This reveals the type of curtain the metaphor is describing. The uniqueness of this metaphor reflects a special characteristic of the expansion itself. With that reference in mind, we need an illustration of a curtain being stretched or opened.

Increased genera follow all ten mass extinctions

That illustration is a top view looking down to a compressed curtain being opened.

Using the curtain illustration of the start of the universe, we picture a closed (compressed) curtain ready to be opened. One normally opens a curtain by grabbing the outer leading edge and pulling it away from the remaining inner compressed body. When the stretching began, the majority of the universe did not move much in the early phases. As time moved on, the outer parts of the universe began to stretch faster than the inner. The illustration below shows a timeline using the curtain metaphor. It is not to scale, but it demonstrates that the early universe expanded more slowly than it does now.

The wave in the illustration below is a top-view curtain image. When opening a curtain, it must be pulled from the end. As it moves along the curtain rod, the end being pulled moves faster. The more it is pulled, the more the remaining curtain opens. The most accelerated stretching is at the outer end being metaphorically pulled.

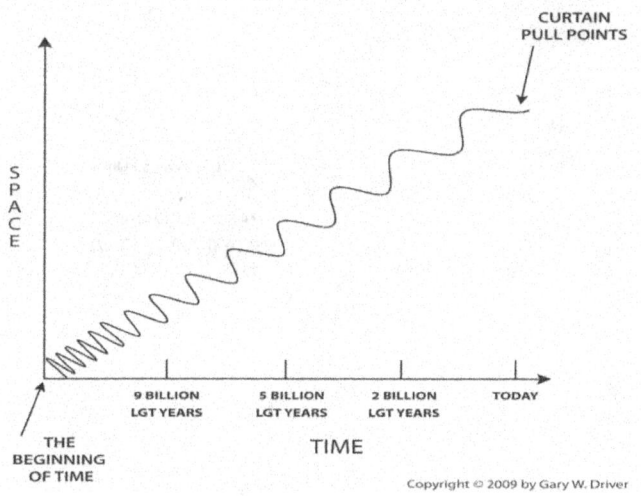

Top view curtain - universe acceleration

An exhaustive study of nearly half a million deformed galaxies observed by the Hubble Space Telescope has provided definitive proof of the acceleration of our universe's expansion. A team of astronomers took a close look at more than 446,000 galaxies observed by Hubble in 557 overlapping photographs—making it the largest survey ever performed by the iconic space telescope. The observations, taken from Hubble's COSMOS study, are the latest confirmation of what scientists have long thought, that a mysterious force called dark energy is driving the universe to not just expand, but to expand at an ever-faster pace.[15]

Adam Riess, Brian Schmidt, and Saul Perlmutter, who were awarded the 2011 Nobel Prize for their discovery, affirmed what the Bible declared in 700 BC: that the universe is indeed accelerating. The illustration below shows the same curatin principle every direction an observer looks. The universe is accelerating faster with greater distance.

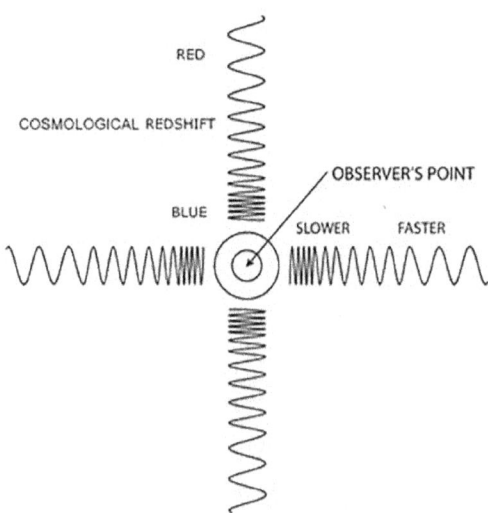

Isotropic view of an accelerating universe.

---

15   "Evidence of the accelerated expansion of the Universe from weak lensing tomography with COSMOS." *Astronomy & Astrophysics*, Volume 516, Article A63 (June 2010).

Increased genera follow all ten mass extinctions

In spite of the accelerating universe, it remains isotropic. This means there is no special location in the universe. The curtain metaphor also demonstrates how an accelerating universe on a very large scale will look regardless of where the observer is located. Everything will appear to be rushing away from him, and the further he looks in all directions, the faster the universe will be moving away.

I have made Earth, and created man upon it: I even my hands, and stretched out the heavens, *and all their host have I commanded.* (Isaiah 45:12)

The curtain metaphor again illustrates the Bible's descriptions of the fabric of space. It shows that it is actually the fabric of space that is being stretched. Picture in your mind that the galaxies and stars are sewn into the fabric of the curtain. By opening the curtain really fast, the sewn galaxies and stars move with the curtain just as the actual galaxies and stars move with the fabric of space. This sheds light on the seeming contradiction that the galaxies are moving faster than the speed of light. It is impossible for light to travel *through* space faster than the cosmological speed limit.

The scripture is not speaking of the universe as a single host (group) but to all, meaning there are many hosts or galaxies. Describing an accelerating universe in 700 BC demonstrates that God is behind dark energy stretching out the universe as if he was pulling on the outer edge of the curtain while holding the galaxies (hosts) and galaxy clusters together using the gravity of the highest order of dust in the universe, dark matter (Proverbs 8:26).

The curtain metaphor reveals not only the accelerating fabric of the universe but also the only method of measuring the expansion, acceleration, and distance of illuminated objects. These are measured by the characteristic of an object's light as it moves toward or away from an observer. This causes the light to compress toward the blue end of the visual spectrum if moving toward us or stretch toward the red end of the spectrum if moving away. Light mirrors the same effect that movement has on sound, which is called the Doppler effect. The Doppler effect is a reference to the changing pitch of a sound-producing object like a siren or horn as it approaches the listener and the different effect it has as it leaves. The sound pitch continues to go up as it approaches the listener, due to the sound waves being compressed, and then goes down in pitch the farther the source moves past the listener as the sound waves are stretched out. In the same way, light waves are compressed when an object moves toward an observer, yielding a light toward the blue end of the spectrum, and light waves are stretched when an illuminated object moves away from an observer, producing a light toward the red end of the spectrum.

> Where is the *way* where light dwelleth? and as for darkness, where is the place thereof. (Job 38:19)

The Bible declares that light does not dwell in a given place; it is always moving. In Job 38:19 the word "way" is the Hebrew word *derek*, which means "road, journey, and distance." The Creator is asking Job to make the distinction between the moving light and the stationary state of darkness. And of course this knowledge was not known, and Job could not answer. The laws of light are the medium to understand the workings of the universe.

The Immeasurable Universe

After 13.8 billion years of expansion, the universe has grown much larger than it once was. In 1948, the theorized afterglow of the Big Bang was estimated to be 5 Kelvin. To make this calculation, two main factors must be known to some degree: the temperature at creation and the expansion rate of the universe. This afterglow called the CMB has been measured to be 2.7 Kelvin. Thus, the universe is finite and getting bigger. At this point in time after creation, it is beyond our visible distance horizon. It's an oxymoron to declare the universe to be infinite and 13.8 billion years old.

> Thus saith the LORD; *If heaven above can be measured,* and the foundations of Earth searched out beneath, I will also cast off all the seed of Israel for all that they have done, saith the LORD. (Jeremiah 31:37)

Before far-reaching telescopes of various types and sizes, instrumentation, radar, lasers, and computers, the Bible predicted the universe could not be measured. The Creator said he was stretching the universe like a curtain, which means it is accelerating faster at the "edges" from any observer's perspective. On the large scale of the universe, the acceleration is faster than the speed of light. Attempting to use light, the fastest thing in the universe, to measure the universe is useless. The light from galaxies that we can see in the distant universe took billions of years to reach the lenses of our telescopes. Thus, the pictures are billions of years old. Some of these galaxies are moving faster than the speed of light and are disappearing from view.

Humankind's visual horizon, which depends upon the speed of light, has absolutely no bearing on the size of the universe. It simply explains why no information beyond that point can travel the opposite direction of the expansion. Unlike the horizon on Earth, which limits our sight because of Earth's curvature, the cosmological horizontal limits are based on straight-line distances.

And because the expansion of space is faster than the speed of light, we will *never* see beyond the region, just as the Creator predicted.

Due to the accelerating expansion, the visual universe is estimated to be 46.5 billion light years in any one direction. If the universe is unimaginably great in size, its Creator must be even greater in ability and capacity. The Creator's prediction is correct once again, verified by science. The universe simply cannot be measured. However, the universe had a beginning a finite time ago, so it certainly cannot be infinite in age or size.

Not until the twentieth century did humankind discover that the universe is larger than the perceived Milky Way galaxy. Not only did Edwin Hubble affirm an expanding universe, he also identified the nearby Andromeda Galaxy and other galaxies as being located beyond our Milky Way. The universe is vastly bigger than anyone anticipated, far larger than the size that we can observe with our telescopes. Certainly, the prophet Jeremiah or any other human in 650 BC would not have had such scientific knowledge. On the surface, this claim of immeasurability seems to contradict God's claim of a universe with a beginning, which implies the universe is finite. Coupled together, the two predictions imply the universe is both finite and too big to be measured, even using the speed of light. This makes God's predictions of both an exponential expansion (Isaiah 42:5a) and an accelerating universe even more credible.

These thoughts raise a question: without the most powerful telescopes, how can any "mortal" know that the universe is immeasurable without being "out there" to access it? Natural beings like humans are limited by the speed of light and space-time. Only a greater than natural (i.e., supernatural) entity is able to make such an assessment of the immeasurable parameters of the universe.

> As the *host of heaven cannot be numbered,* neither the sand of the sea measured. (Jeremiah 33:22a)

The Bible also asserts that the stars and galaxies (the host of heaven) in the universe cannot be numbered. The stars in the Milky Way alone cannot be numbered. Neither can the galaxies in the universe. And the stars in each of those innumerable galaxies cannot be numbered. At the time of this biblical prediction, on a clear night, an Earth-bound observer could see about twenty-five hundred stars. Looking at the night sky with the naked eye will not lead anyone to think the visible stars can not be counted or that there are any hosts called galaxies. Astronomers *estimate* that the Milky Way contains up to four hundred *billion* stars. There are giant galaxies that contain more than a *trillion* stars. Astronomers *estimate* there are one hundred to three hundred *billion* such galaxies in the observable universe. Once again, the Creator predicted another attribute of the universe he created, verified by science.

Physicists also discuss the notion of the "multiverse," which theorizes that there are an innumerable number of universes. As many as 10^{500} have been proposed, with the idea of a quasi-*infinite* number of universes, each containing any and all parameters, physical laws, constants, values, and any possible combination thereof, thus eliminating the uniqueness of the universe we observe. Ironically, if *all possible* universes exist in a multiverse scenario, one of them must be a created universe by the God of the Bible. Not only does the Bible predict the universe is immeasurable, it also declares all the worlds (universes) are framed by God.

> Through faith we understand that the worlds were framed by the word of God, so that things which are seen were not made of things which do appear. (Hebrews 11:3)

If there are multiple universes, the Bible declares the worlds were framed by the word of God. The point is that there is a reference to more than one world. What kind of world the Bible is referring to, either angelic or natural, is not known. Nor does the proposed multiverse give any hint as to the kind of existence it contains. The existence or nonexistence of the multiverse, supersymmetry, string theory, or other Earthlike planets with extra-terrestrials have no effect on the predictions of the Bible and the observable universe we call home. There is no scientific evidence of another universe; an infinite number of universes are quite a stretch. If there are multiple universes out there, it is totally irrelevant to the predictions of the Bible. This is the universe in which the Creator instructs us to look for verification of his handiwork.

Lift up your eyes on high, and behold who hath created these things. (Isaiah 40:26a)

This vastness of the universe has been cited by materialists as evidence that humanity on this small obscure planet is not special in relation to the universe. Materialists hold a world view in which all existence consists of matter and is the source of all consciences, thoughts, and morals. In addition, all phenomena have only physical explanations. This is often coupled with the ancient notion that humanity is special because the Earth was considered to be the center of the universe. Before Copernicus revealed the sun was the center of the known universe, both science and religion (i.e., everybody) had the same belief. It was error by religion to base the value of humanity upon the perceived space-time location of Earth. It is the same error for materialists today to base the value of humanity on the vastness of the universe.

To get a better understanding of this human value, let's consider how the value of an expensive commodity (say, a Rolls Royce) is accessed. A Rolls Royce automobile is indeed very expensive and a rare sight on the roadway. The high price is determined by the engineering, design, craftsmanship, labor, and quality of material used to make it. In order to purchase one of these automobiles, the input that it took to create it, plus profit, has to be paid. Thus, the value is determined by what is put into the automobile.

Humanity is no different when considering what it took to create us. First, the natural aspect of humanity was created from the star dust of several generations of stars, as Genesis 2:4 declares. Many stars died for there to be the elements of which we are made. Many plants and animals died so that we can have fossil fuel for our lives. The eternal spiritual souls of all humans are a product of God himself who gave them. The same God of all creation was established via his natural laws; there is no free lunch. He has placed the ultimate value on humanity by the price he required be paid to redeem us from his spiritual laws, which we had breached. That price to redeem humanity required God to go above all creation to obtain the only entity capable of paying the price God set forth to redeem humanity, none other than the son of God and co-Creator, Jesus. Jesus could not use his inherent riches to redeem humanity; God required him to freely give his life. The price paid to redeem us in part reflects what it took to create us to be both natural and eternal. We are indeed special.

Nine billion years after the creation of the universe in Genesis 1:1, we arrive to the birth of our solar system which starts with Genesis 1:2.

Chapter 4

The Days of Our Solar System

When researching the Genesis creation narrative, it is good to know that it is not a comprehensive account; rather, it represents major events or milestones in the creation journey. Many people in the church community fixate on the discussion of the "days" in Genesis. Many are convinced that any interpretation other than the most literal one compromises God's word. However, it is the Bible that instructs both believers and unbelievers in Isaiah 40:26 to look to the heavens as a witness of God as Creator. By refusing to examine the science (knowledge) of the heavens is to ignore or disobey the very scripture we purport to support. Looking to the stars is a reference to the science of light in its many wavelengths. The light literally allows us to look back in time, revealing the phenomena and character of the universe, as well as its age.

> *Lift up your eyes on high, and behold who hath created these things,* That bringeth out their host by number: (Isaiah 40:26a)

> *Lift up your eyes to the heavens, and look upon Earth beneath:* for the heavens shall vanish away like smoke, and Earth shall wax old like a garment. (Isaiah 51:6a)

The generations of the heavens referred to in Genesis 2:4 cover time from the initial creation to the formation of our solar system. Thus, the first nine billion years must be considered part of the first day. Genesis 2:4b reads, "in the day that the Lord God made the earth and the heavens." This "day" is the sum total of all creation, including the plants on the Earth and humans.

> Where wast thou when I laid the foundations of the Earth? declare, if thou hast understanding. Who hath laid the measures thereof, if thou knowest? or who hath stretched the line upon it? Whereupon are the foundations thereof fastened? or who laid the corner stone thereof; *When the morning stars sang together,* and all the sons of God shouted for joy? (Job 38:4-7)

Based in part upon Job 38:4-7, I conclude that Genesis 1:2 is a reference to the formation of our solar system. In God's rebuke of Job, he refers to the shining of stars that was occurring at the time he began forming the foundations of Earth. This suggests there were stars and galaxies as outlined in Chapter Three. Job 38:7 is biblical affirmation of what occurred before Genesis 1:2. The cornerstone represents the first laid stone in a building process and is a critical structural point. This start in the laying out of the foundation of the Earth compares with Genesis 1:2 in its reference to the Earth being without form and void. The morning stars sang when the foundations of the Earth were being laid.

Increased genera follow all ten mass extinctions

So who are the morning stars? Some Bible commentators suggest the morning stars and the sons of God are both a reference to the angels. Some suggest the morning stars are a reference to literal stars and the sons of God is a reference to the angels. I agree with the latter, that the morning stars are literal stars because of the conjunction "and" between the morning stars and the sons of God. The "and" indicates they are not one and the same entity. Job 38:7 declares when the stars sang together; this poetically speaks of harmony in shining. The only thing the stars do is shine. Thus, the formation of the Earth began after stars were shining.

According to the Big Bang theory, Earth was formed about nine billion years after the original creation. Many of the Christian faith believe the universe was created in seven literal days. Genesis chapter one is often cited as evidence of this; when each of the first six days are concluded with the phrase, the "evening and morning" was that particular day. This phrase's explanation is usually limited to a twenty-four-hour period.

> And the vision of the evening and the morning which was told is true: wherefore shut thou up the vision; for it shall be for many days. (Daniel 8:26)

The vision is the time duration of all the following empires:

The Babylon Empire	(605–539 BC)
The Media-Persia Empire	(539–331 BC)
The Greek Empire	(331–168 BC)
The Roman Empire	(168 BC–AD 476)
The Divided Kingdom	(AD 476–NOW)
Christ's Kingdom	(??–Eternity)

Thus, according to the Bible, evening and morning is certainly not limited to one twenty-four-hour day. The phrase evening and morning is the beginning and end of an undetermined time period. At this point in time, the phrase in Daniel refers to over twenty-five hundred years to date. This conclusion is not based upon "science."

The Bible uses the stars to give a reference to a long-time duration from the original creation to the universe observed today. The Book of Psalms 19 says that the heavens in general declare the glory of God through his creation. In the context of his glorious handiwork, verses four through six describe in particular a metaphor of our sun. First, the Creator has set or established a tabernacle or dwelling place for the sun. Until recent scientific discovery revealed the sun actually revolves around the Milky Way galaxy, the metaphorical meaning of the tabernacle was unclear. Verse five further describes the sun as a bridegroom coming out of his chamber. To unpack the metaphor, one must first unpack the characteristics of the bridegroom chamber.

First the bridegroom chamber is where the marriage is consummated. According to the wedding traditions of the time, the bride and groom would enter the provided chamber and consummate the marriage while certain invited members of the wedding waited outside. An example is found in John 3:29. After consummation, the bridegroom would come out and announce the consummation had been completed, thus making them legally married.

The private bridegroom chamber is synonymous with the coming together of elements to form a star in the hidden chamber of nebulous space dust clouds. This start of our sun is how stars are born. The running of a race refers to the speed that the sun travels in the orbit of its galaxy (tabernacle). Thus, the Bible figuratively proclaims the lengthy birth process of stars.

The Bible also addresses the death of stars in Isaiah 34:4, describing the falling of stars as witnessed with the timely falling

Increased genera follow all ten mass extinctions

of each vine leaf and the falling of each fig on a tree. Thus, the Bible affirms the life and death of stars in Psalm 19:4-6 and Isaiah 34:4.

> And all the host of heaven shall be dissolved, and the heavens shall be rolled together as a scroll: and all their host shall fall down, as the leaf falleth off from the vine, and as a falling fig from the fig tree. (Isaiah 34:4)

Stars have a life span: they are born, live, and die. And they that dwell on Earth shall die in like manner, as the Creator has designated the fate of the stars from the initial creation. Couple this understanding with the knowledge that the seed (elements) of previous stars are part of newborn stars. This establishes there are generations of stars. Our sun, for example, is a third-generation star, based upon its element content.

Starting near the end in this Genesis creation narrative account allows scripture to give us understanding. The Genesis creation narrative actually ends in chapter two, including this summary statement:

> These are the generations of the heavens and of Earth when they were created, in the day that the LORD God made Earth and the heavens. (Genesis 2:4)

Due to the placement of Genesis 2:4 at the end of the narrative, it is often overlooked, regarded as an insignificant closing remark and misinterpreted at times as an introduction of a genealogical reference to humans. This scripture references all of the previous scriptures of the narrative events that occurred through the days (periods) of creation as a whole. Genesis 2:4 is the same as Genesis 1:1 in the use of the words heavens and Earth. In Genesis 2:4, the *entire* process is described as a single day (time) in which God created the heavens and Earth. But "the day" really refers to the sum of the previous seven days. It is impossible for one day to be equal to six days, if all of the Genesis references to days are to twenty-four-hour days.

In Genesis 2:4, the Hebrew word *toldah,* translated as "generations," means descendants. It is also used in Genesis 5:1 to refer to the generations of Adam. Some Bible translations use the word "account" in place of "generations." Again, by examining the stars (as instructed in Isaiah 51:6) research has discovered the stars live and die like the creatures on Earth, and the remnant elements (seed) become new stars. The Bible declares the stars are created (born) in the nebular in Psalm 19:5. "Generations" indeed mean an account of the descendants.

The generations of the heavens are of the stars that live and die. We are commanded to look into the heavens to see the glory of our Lord and understand what they speak. Due to the abundance of heavy elements in our solar system, scientists have determined our sun is a third-generation star. Earth is also a part of these generations, formed in the same accretion disk as the sun. Everything in verse four is actually a part of these generations of stars, which can add up to billions of years. Their life and death have given seed for the next generation of stars, which will live and die, and the life cycle will continue. The elements used by the Creator to form Earth came from the generations of the stars, and the Creator used the dust of the ground to form Adam.

We have heard scientists declare that "we are all star dust," often in a derisive way that implies that we were not created as the Bible proclaims. Yet, without knowledge of the scriptures, they have unwittingly affirmed what the Bible predicted: the Earth, as well as everything on it, is star dust.

Increased genera follow all ten mass extinctions

The context of Genesis 2:1–3 is the seventh day and the heavens and Earth, which God created. Again, he states that *in or within* the seventh day (eon), he ended his work and rested. Unlike the previous six days, the seventh makes no mention of evening or morning. The end of the sixth day implies the beginning of a seventh day with no reference to an end of that seventh day.

Exodus 20:11 is quoted often as evidence that the creation was done in six literal twenty-four-hour days. The verse reads: "For *in* six days the LORD made heaven and Earth, the sea, and all that in them *is*, and rested the seventh day: wherefore the LORD blessed the Sabbath day, and hallowed it." The preposition "in" was added to the original writing during the translation from Hebrew to English in the King James Version. Removing "in" alters the meaning and indicates a simple duration of six days.

The same preposition "in" was added to Exodus 31:17 with the same result. The sum of the work in Exodus 20:11 and 31:17 states that this was made; the word created was not used. There is no proof Exodus was referring to twenty-four-hour days. The reference that God uses for his own work period is not an exact reflection, but a similitude for us to follow in our twenty-four-hour-a-day workweek. While Exodus 20:11 is a correct general statement, Genesis 2:2-4 is more precise, referring to the sum of all God's work of the generations of the heaven and Earth, both of which he created. We find the same is said of the making of Earth in Isaiah 45:18.

> For thus saith the LORD that created the heavens; God himself that formed the Earth and made it; he hath established it, he created it not in vain, he formed it to be inhabited: I am the LORD; and there is none else. (Isaiah 45:18)

The Creator describes a process that Earth went through. First, it was formed, meaning molded or fashioned, as something that is malleable, reflecting Genesis 1:2, being without form and void, or empty and incomplete. It was then made to be what he intended. Then he established it by providing stability to what was not stable. Thus, the creation of Earth was not instantaneous or without purpose. Again, he fashioned it to be inhabited with life. There was certainly a time in which the Earth was not inhabitable if the Creator needed to make it inhabitable. This is in accord with the lengthy time needed to make it inhabitable that is supported by scientific fact.

While man was created on day six, generations of humans cannot be obtained from the six days if they are literal twenty-four-hour days, if the reference is to human generations. That leaves one twenty-four-hour day for descendants to produce generations. Thus, the generations are not a reference to humans but to the stars and planets. The sum of days reflected the principle of God's resting after a period of work. God determined the milestone time frames we call days because his work ended on the seventh day, as the passage proclaims.

This is another scriptural reference that does not compare to the literal twenty-four-hour day, which occurs within the third day, as proclaimed in Genesis 1:11. God commanded to allow (let) the Earth to bring forth the grass, herbs, and trees along with its seed to be produced after its kind. After he had made this declaration, he said it was so. In verse twelve, God said for the second time to affirm that it was the Earth indeed that brought forth the grass, herbs, and fruit after its kind. This describes the multiplying of the vegetation by way of producing seed, which in turn produced more vegetation. The Earth could not bring forth these generations of vegetation in one day.

This is yet another scripture in Genesis that does not accord with a twenty-four-hour day. On the sixth day, God created both Adam and Eve, male and female, along with all the animals. In Genesis 2:7-22, God provides more details of day six. In Genesis 2:7, God reaffirms the creation of Adam from the dust of the ground. The plants and trees were created back on day three. In verse eight, God started the natural process of planting the previously created seeds, plants, and trees in the garden of Eden. He placed Adam there to dress and keep the garden that has grown naturally *out of the ground*, according to verse nine. These trees of verse nine that God caused to grow out of the ground did not grow in one literal day.

Before he could direct his attention to the growing garden, Adam had a job to do in naming all the animals. Yes, all of them: every beast of the field, all the fowl of the air, all bovine animals, all living creatures. During this laborious naming process, Adam did not find a helpmate for him to be capable of reproducing after his kind. Then God caused Adam to fall into a deep sleep to form Eve from his own body. The natural process of planting and growing of the garden, along with naming of all creatures, certainly took more than a twenty-four-hour day.

The First Day—Hadean Eon

> And Earth was without form, and void; and darkness was upon the face of the deep. And the Spirit of God moved upon the face of the waters. (Genesis 1:2)

Verse two starts with the formation of our solar system and the Hadean Eon. The Hadean Eon is the first period of time on Earth's geological time scale, starting 4.6 billion years ago. Cosmologists have a theory for the formation of our solar system called the nebular model. The observations of other planetary systems shed some light on our solar system. The following features give some understanding that the solar system was formed as a unit.

First, all planets move around the sun in the same direction. Second, the inner orbiting planets are rocky, denser, and smaller than the large, gaseous outer planets. Third, every planet has a relatively flat orbital inclination to the sun. Modern telescopes have allowed scientists to examine the growth stages of solar systems throughout the universe with a proto star in the midst of a spinning disk of dust and gas. These observations form the basis of the nebular theory.

The above scripture describes the point in creation when Earth did not have the form it has today, being empty and unfit for life. Observable evidence shows the heavier, rock-based planets formed closer to the center of this orbiting activity. Mercury, Venus, Earth, and Mars are rocky planets, while the remaining planets in the outer solar system are more gaseous. All of the planets were in the process of being formed concurrently, along with the sun in its formation process while in the nebula. Before the sun became a light-producing star, darkness was indeed upon the face of the deep, an Earth covered with water.

Earth's initial form was not what we observe today. The spirit of God moving upon the face of the Earth is reflective of God's hand in his creation. Hebrews 1:10 (below) also reflects the works of God's hands on the heavens and Earth. Thus, both Genesis 1:2 and Hebrews 1:10 offer metaphors of God intervening in the creation of the universe. These are not references to creation out of nothing. The generations of the heavens were made according to a desired outcome, as a potter forms the clay.

> And, Thou, Lord, in the beginning hast laid the foundation of the Earth; and the heavens are the works of thine hands. (Hebrews 1:10)

Increased genera follow all ten mass extinctions

> It is turned as clay to the seal; and they stand as a garment. (Job 38:14)

In Job 38:14, God questions Job concerning his ability to create the world around him, highlighting Job's lack of authority and power to do the same. The Earth is said to be "turned." The word turned is the Hebrew word *haphak*, which means "to change." In this metaphor, the clay is in a malleable state to be formed by the seal, which is the Hebrew word *chowtham*, meaning "signet." The foundation of the Earth was without form; however, it was malleable like other round planets, whose round shape was influenced by the force of gravity. Due to the weakness of gravity, all the round planets, stars, and other round objects were at some point in time in a malleable state for gravity to produce such consistent spheres. Even today the foundation(s) of the Earth are in a hot, malleable state. Volcanoes are evidence of molten rock beneath Earth's crust. The Bible indicates that the Earth was in a malleable condition, the same hot, molten condition theorized by scientists to have existed during the Hadean Eon, which comes from the word Hades. Therefore, the Creator is proclaiming the foundation and the outer crust or garment had an intended outcome, as the use of the signet had an intended outcome upon the clay. The outer garment will be addressed in the section on tectonic plates.

> I beheld the Earth, and, lo, it was without form, and void; and the heavens, and they had no light. (Jeremiah 4:23)

This is a sparse creation reference in which the Creator declares that the disobedient nation does not know him and what he is capable of. Verse 23 is a reference to God's power to change the

Earth from its early lack of form to the later formations during a time before there was light in our solar system.

The Creator proclaimed the existence of water on Earth when it was new. Scientists estimate that water was on Earth in the Hadean Eon. Earth is indeed unique in its abundance of water compared to the other planets in our solar system. Earth was formed to be inhabited, as stated in Isaiah 45:18. This did not hold much weight at the time of this claim's historical record, when humankind's knowledge was limited to Earth. Now we can observe the cosmos with powerful telescopes that reveal that, so far, Earth is one of a kind in many life-sustaining ways. Now the claim speaks volumes in its reference to the early time in which water was present and to the uniqueness of Earth's abundant water supply.

Who laid the foundations of Earth, that it should not be removed forever. Thou coveredst it with the deep as with a garment: the waters stood above the mountains. (Psalm 104:5–6)

Again, the Earth is correctly described as having more than one foundation that is immoveable and internal. The early Earth was covered with the deep as proclaimed in Genesis 1:2. The oddest part of this verse is the claim that the waters stood above the mountains. Like sea-floor spreading in plate tectonic activity, only in the deep ocean one can witness such a phenomenon. Of course, no one could identify anything in the depths of the oceans. The largest single geographical feature on Earth is the Mid-Atlantic Ridge created by sea-floor spreading.

Water covers about two-thirds of Earth's surface, and it is vital for the survival of all living creatures. Some scientists have hypothesized that water was transferred here by asteroids and comets. However, the sheer amount of water needed, and why Earth received and retained such a large amount relative to the other planets, doesn't seem plausible as a coincidence. Despite having the simple composition of H_2O, no one has found a safe way to create an abundant supply of water on Earth. The combination of the two violent, combustible chemicals, hydrogen and oxygen, make it difficult. Most liquid fuel rocket engines, and the three main, high-thrust engines of the NASA space shuttles using a combination of liquid hydrogen and oxygen as fuel, gives a good indication of the volatility of such a combination. The two fuels were kept separated in fuel tanks and blended in the engines just before ignition.

Water is the only natural substance that occurs in all three states of solid, liquid, and gas. It expands when it freezes, causing ice to float, which is essential for aquatic life. If it did not expand, ice would sink to the bottom and cause the remaining water to freeze, killing all aquatic life. By freezing on top, the ice insulates the water beneath, allowing the underwater life to survive. Water is truly the most wonderful substance on Earth due to all of the ways it contributes to the function of Earth and life. Someday, scientists might figure out conclusively how water was made on the early Earth.

> Where wast thou when I laid the *foundations* of the Earth? declare, if thou hast understanding. Who hath laid the measures thereof, if thou knowest? or who hath stretched the line upon it? Whereupon are the *foundations* thereof fastened? or who laid the corner stone thereof; When the morning stars sang together, and all the sons of God shouted for joy? (Job 38:4-7)

The Bible actually declares the Earth was created after stars were formed. After the process of creation of "morning stars," the foundations of Earth were formed. The morning stars are stars like our sun. Here the Bible declares the sun is a star. The morning stars are said to sing together, which means they act in unison in the only thing they do: to shine. For stars to already exist in the state of shining means a long time had transpired after the initial creation of the universe before the formation of Earth began.

Consideration must be made that at the time of the writing of the Old Testament's scriptural references to morning stars, our sun was not accepted to be actually a star. After the record of scripture, the sun was first suggested to be a star around 450 BC. In addition, the morning stars shining before Earth was formed suggest that the later reference of "let there be light" does not refer to the first light of the universe, but to the beginning of our sun. The verse speaks of the morning stars and the sons of God as two different entities by the use of the conjunction "and." These are the same sons of the God of Job 1:6. It also lets us know that this angelic host (sons of God) was created before Earth was formed. The opportunity for the fall of Satan was long before the Garden of Eden and the fall of Adam.

The foundations of Earth evince a process of construction. The use of the plural "foundations" is because there are several foundations or layers to its composition. Just as a house has layers of foundations, so does Earth. In the construction of a home, the first foundation is the ground on which the second foundation, usually concrete, is laid. As shown in the picture below, Earth also has two foundations: the solid inner iron alloy core, and the liquid outer iron core. The inner core actually rotates within the outer core at a rate faster than the outer crust rotates on its axis. This is theorized to generate the magnetic field around Earth, which protects it from the sun's solar wind.

Increased genera follow all ten mass extinctions

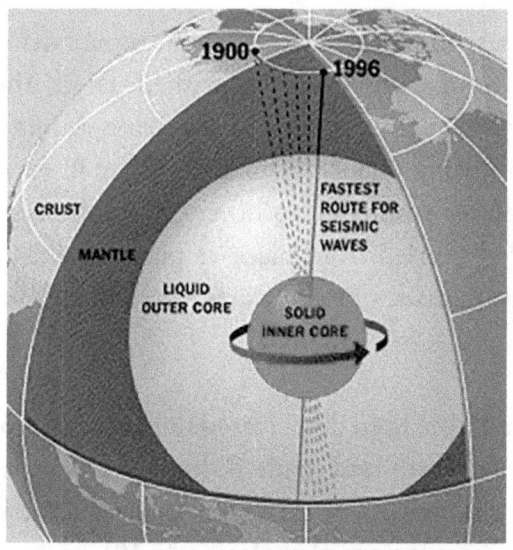

Earth's foundations, NASA image

The burden of the word of the LORD for Israel, saith the LORD, which stretcheth forth the heavens, and <u>layeth</u> the foundation of the Earth, and formeth the spirit of man within him. (Zechariah 12:1)

Layer upon layer, God added to Earth's foundations. God did not create Earth in a twenty-four-hour day. This took a long time; it is the continual process of the sun's creation that God described in Psalm 19. Just as God opened the sky for us to see his glory in the cosmos, he has literally opened Earth for us to see firsthand his handiwork in forming our planet. I am speaking of one particular great natural site called the Grand Canyon, whose spectacular array of layers (strata) of different rock and soil shows the changes and growth of Earth over time. Some formations are the same throughout the canyon, which is, of course, grand. Other sites around the world which reveal these strata are both the same and quite different.

Within these time-based strata are the remains (fossils) of land-based and sea animals. (We will deal with life later.) This also affirms that Earth was actually formed, as the Bible claims. Preservation of minor, and some major, formations differ in various amounts from some places compared to others. Conditions at the time of formation likely varied from place to place. The claim that Earth has a foundation made of many parts has been affirmed by science.

> For thus said the Lord that created the heavens; God himself that formed Earth *and* made it; he had *established* it, and created it not in vain, he formed it to be inhabited: I am the Lord and there is none else. (Isaiah 45:18)

God is claiming he made Earth. The word "made" here is translated from the Hebrew word *asah*, which means "to fashion." This is the same Hebrew word used in Genesis 6:6 in his description of how he made humans on Earth from the dust of the ground. God took the material he brought together when he formed Earth to make it the way he wanted and needed to create life. This also coincides with Genesis 2:4. Earth is made from the material of the generations of the heavens (stars). The Earth is unique in all the attributes it has to facilitate life. Regardless if there are billions of earthlike planets discovered in the universe, the Bible is referring to the one we live on.

A Star Is Born

> And God said, Let there be light: and there was light. And God saw the light, that it was good: and God divided the light from the darkness. And God called the light Day,

and the darkness he called Night. And the evening and the morning were the *first day*. (Genesis 1:3–5)

Genesis 1:2 ends with darkness on the face of the deep, which is not a reference to darkness everywhere. Due to the number of heavy elements found on Earth and other planets, our sun is not a first-generation star. It is estimated to be a third-generation star. Other stars had died to provide the quantity of life-giving elements to form our solar system. Our sun was born in a nebula or chamber of creation, as described later in Psalm 19:5. Our sun, as the new protostar, started its stellar nucleosynthesis and produced light, announcing its birth to the universe. God said, "Let there be light," and there was light for the solar system. This same process that produces light had been going on in other stars in the universe; however, this verse refers specifically to the star of our solar system, which contains the Earth.

In the representative image below, the nucleosynthesis began in the center of the accretion disk that formed our solar system.

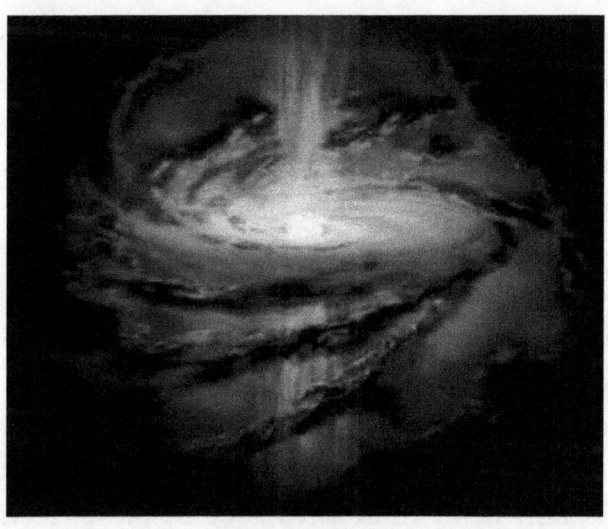

A Star is born, NASA image

Light is photons that have been released by the electrons of atoms. For light to continue to shine, it has to be continually produced. Light was not created in the same sense as creating some object with mass like the Earth. When the conditions according to those laws are met, light is produced.

> I form the light, and create darkness: I make peace, and create evil: I the LORD do all these things. (Isaiah 45:7)

The above scripture declares that light is formed in the present tense. The Hebrew word *yatsar* is translated as "to form." It refers to the action of a potter or maker to create or frame. It is an excellent parallel with the actual production of light in that both require energy or a force to be applied to produce both light and the pottery. Light is produced when a quantized amount of energy is added to an atom; the electron(s) are thus excited and move to a higher orbit. To discharge the energy that was added, the electron(s) move back to a lower orbit and discharge a packet of energy (photon) in the form of light. This process must continue for light to continue to shine. When the energy being added to the atoms stops, the atoms stop producing light, and darkness is the product. This also reflects the present tense of the Creator's proclamation about forming light and creating darkness. This motif continues in this scripture with peace and evil; energy is required to maintain peace, as it is with light. And when that effort stops, evil fills the void left by the absence of peace, just as darkness fills the void left by the absence of light.

When a star is born, nuclear fusion begins, and this blast clears the surrounding area of the dust that allows the new star to shine. It was a healthy newborn declared good by the Creator. The sun subsequently begins its way into the main sequence observed today.

Increased genera follow all ten mass extinctions

Day and night are relative to Earth's rotation. When Earth began to rotate is not known. The Creator labeled Earth's exposure to the sun "day" and the subsequent non-exposure "night." The word "day" is translated from the Hebrew word *yome*. It is also translated in other areas of the Bible to the English words "time, day, year, ever, continually," and other temporal meanings. This means it can be any time duration unit, from a twenty-four-hour day to an eon. The reference to evening and morning are the start and finish of an event in time. The Creator has not informed us precisely what that time duration was, along with a lot other mysterious secrets he has kept to himself. This is the end of a period that only the Creator knows. This time period and the other day-referenced scripture of Genesis 1 will be labeled an eon, because the Creator himself has established the time to create the heavenly bodies of his universe, which includes Earth. If we ignore other scriptures pertaining to creation to defend a concept, then the concept becomes more important than the scriptures. It is the Creator who has instructed us to observe the heavens, which reveal his work and character and speak every language known to humankind so that we can obtain knowledge of him.

To take a proper look at his handiwork requires different kinds of powerful telescopes along with sophisticated equipment and the expertise to operate them. The data will speak for itself; to ignore the data is to ignore scripture and the results of the observation we are to use in order to determine who created the universe, and to rob God of his glory. The Eagle Nebula shown below is an example of the glory God predicted as the birthplace of stars as outlined in Psalms 19.

Eagle Nebula – "Pillars of Creation" NASA Hubble Space Telescope

The heavens declare the glory of God; and the firmament sheweth his handywork. Day unto day uttereth speech, and night unto night sheweth knowledge. There is no speech nor language, where their voice is not heard. Their line is gone out through all Earth, and their words to the end of the world. In them hath he set a tabernacle for the sun, Which is as a bridegroom *coming out of his chamber,* and rejoiceth as a strong man to run a race. (Psalm 19:1–5)

Like a strong man rejoicing, the Creator describes the sun as being strong and full of energy. Scientists estimate the sun has about seven billion years' worth of fuel to make thirty-one orbits of the Milky Way, taking about two hundred twenty-five million years to complete each orbit. The word "run" is translated from the Hebrew word *ruwts,* which means "to run swiftly." The word "race" is translated from the Hebrew word *orach,* which means "a pathway or highway." Considering these two words, a more precise meaning from the original Hebrew language yields a prediction of a *fast* path or highway.

The sun orbits the Milky Way galaxy at an abnormal 520,000 miles per hour with its planets in tow. And while the sun is blazing around the galaxy, the galaxy itself is moving through space at 1.3 million miles per hour, relative to the CMB radiation that permeates the universe. The psalmist certainly could not have known these attributes of the galaxy and of the sun. How could such knowledge be obtained by the illiterate peasants of King David's time? In addition, the Bible also predicts the sun's going forth from the end of heaven, which refers to a long distance, like the saying "from here to heaven." The sun traveling at 520,000 miles per hour takes 220 million years to make one orbit. It takes light traveling at 186,000 miles per second 100,000 *years* to go from one side of the Milky Way to the other. That's certainly from here to heaven in terms of our distance perspective. The sheer size of the Milky Way contributed to the long-held theory that it constituted the entire universe until Hubble affirmed otherwise, confirming the tremendous size of the tabernacle of the sun called the Milky Way galaxy.

> His going forth is from the *end of the heaven,* and his *circuit unto the ends of it:* and there is nothing hid from the heat thereof. (Psalm 19:6)

Finally, in verse six, the Creator predicts the path or highway of our sun as a circuit with ends. A circuit or circle with ends is an elliptical shape. In the scriptural context of the tabernacle or galaxy, a varied degree of elliptical orbits (eccentricity) of our sun and stars are found to orbit black holes at the center of galaxies.

The most common orbits in the universe are elliptical. Planetary orbits around the sun have an elliptical shape. Earth travels 67,000 miles per hour in its elliptical orbit around the sun, which itself is traveling at 520,000 miles per hour in a slightly elliptical orbit around the Milky Way, at whose center lies a supermassive black hole. Yes, the Bible predicted elliptical orbits.

The Second Day—Archean Eon

> And God said, Let there be a firmament in the midst of the waters, and let it divide the waters from the waters. And God made the firmament, and divided the waters which were under the firmament from the waters which were above the firmament: and it was so. And God called the firmament Heaven. And the evening and the morning were the *second day*. (Genesis 1:6–8)

God didn't merely make Earth; he established it for the purpose of habitation, as stated in Isaiah 45:18. This required an atmosphere with the necessary combination of elements needed for life. The word "established" is translated from the Hebrew word *kuwn*, which means "to prepare, make ready." After the extremely long Hadean Eon, Earth had a crust and cooled with an unknown atmosphere that needed to be formed. Earth's current atmosphere is composed of nitrogen (78 percent), oxygen (21 percent), argon (1 percent), and trace amounts of other elements. Lower altitudes also have quantities of water vapor.

By the start of the Archean Eon, Earth's crust had cooled. The atmosphere was composed of volcanic gases, including

Increased genera follow all ten mass extinctions

nitrogen, hydrogen, carbon, and possibly low levels of oxygen. Water vapor was abundant and the first oceans had formed.[16]

Genesis 2:4-6 paints the picture of a barren Earth: the atmosphere (firmament) was not created and there was no seed in the ground, there was not yet a rain cycle, the Earth was a misty place, and no man was there. During the formation of vital processes and attributes needed for life, the Earth was not ready for man. Then the account of the creation of man begins at Genesis 2:7.

> And every plant of the field before it was in the Earth, and every herb of the field before it grew: for the LORD God had not caused it to rain upon the Earth, and there was not a man to till the ground. But there went up a mist from the Earth, and watered the whole face of the ground. (Genesis 2:5-6)

During this epoch, the sun and other chemical influences changed the existing gases of the volatile planet into the mixtures needed for life. God claimed to create the layers of the atmosphere (firmament) in Amos 9:6 below. This is a layered atmospheric dome extending sixty-two hundred miles above the surface of the Earth.

> It is he that buildeth his *stories* in the heaven, and hath founded his troop in Earth; he that calleth for the waters of

---

[16] Smithsonian National Museum of Natural History, "The Archaean," http://paleobiology.si.edu

the sea, and poureth them out upon the face of Earth: The Lord is his name. (Amos 9:6)

The timelines of Earth's early history are difficult to determine precisely. However, it is understood that Earth's atmosphere did not pop into existence; it developed over time, starting in the Archean Eon. Amos 9:6 refers to the "stories" of heaven where rain is produced and poured upon Earth. The word "stories" is the Hebrew word *ma'alah*, which means "degrees, steps, or stairs." The stories are the atmosphere that the Creator founded or established. The word translated as "to troop" means "bands or binding, vault of heavens, the fitting together of the firmament." The firmament is a solid dome of gases, and the stories (layers of the atmosphere) were built as steps, one upon another as is the atmosphere of Earth. These stories are essential to the process of rain just as the scripture describes and will be discussed in detail later. This scripture also describes the building of those atmospheric layers, which happened during the early formation of Earth.

All of the naturally occurring elements of the periodic table, with the exception of hydrogen and helium, were created in the life and death process of the stars within the nine billion years leading up to this time before Earth's formation. In the process of the life and death of the stars, the Creator established the universe's first recycling program. Those elements were used by the Creator to form the atmosphere.

It took some time for the atmosphere to get to a thermally balanced point when the upper atmosphere would condense water and the lower atmosphere evaporated from the heat of the sun. The water that is suspended continually in the upper atmosphere is separated from the water on Earth. Analysis of ancient rocks indicates low oxygen levels on Earth during its early formation (around about 2.3 billion years ago, according to analysis of rocks that contain traces of oxygen). The establishment of light from the new sun and the formation of Earth's atmosphere set the stage for the support of life that would increase the amount of oxygen in the atmosphere. The formation of the atmosphere (firmament) in the second eon by the master builder (Creator) establishes the foundation of Earth's water cycle, protection from solar radiation, and meteorites.

The Third Day—Proterozoic Eon

> And God said, Let the waters under the heaven be gathered together unto one place, and let the dry land appear: and it was so. And God called the dry land Earth; and the gathering together of the waters called the Seas: and God saw that it was good. (Genesis 1:9–10)

The watery start that characterized the first two biblical eons is about to change. The next major aspect of this journey of creation described in the Bible is the formation of the continents. The Bible states that at one time in Earth's history, the water was gathered into one place, and then the dry land, which was possibly formed by accretion, began to appear out of the body of water. After a long process, a large supercontinent called Rodinia (a Russian term meaning "motherland") was formed. This was not the only proposed supercontinent, but it is thought to be the first. The time scale of the formation of these land masses is not certain; however, geologists can determine the commonality of different land masses and conclude they were indeed connected. The Bible predicted the land mass was formed and appeared out of the water.

> Who laid the foundations of Earth, that it should not be removed for ever. Thou coveredst it with the deep as with a garment: the waters stood above the mountains. At thy rebuke they fled; at the voice of thy thunder they hasted away. (Psalm 104:5-7)

Out of the midst of a water-covered planet, the land was brought forth. God's rebuke is an assertion of his authority over the natural world by bringing forth the continents, and the water, as it were, fled. Not only did he bring together the land on the face of the planet, the Creator also divided the continents. As proclaimed later in reference to the prediction of seafloor spreading and continental drift, the Creator is the one who is controlling the plate tectonics on Earth. There is no question that the continents are moving constantly, as confirmed by researchers, who can monitor land movement in real time. GPS sensors around the globe constantly monitor both the lateral and vertical movements of the continents, which are moving apart and grinding against each other, causing earthquakes and forming mountains.

The concept of continental drift is not new. It was first proposed by Alfred Wegener in his 1915 book called *The Origin of Continents and Oceans*. Typical of the discovery of new phenomena, his work was not accepted by the scientific community at the time due to lack of causal evidence. Then, he obtained evidence of the movement of the continents. He located tropical plant fossils in the arctic regions and sea fossils in the mountains. Almost all mountain ranges have sea fossils at high elevations, which were once on the floor of the sea. It was not until the 1960s when technology allowed scientists to investigate the ocean floor with unmanned submarines that mountain ridges were discovered in the dark depth of the oceans. This led to the discovery of tectonic plates as the causal reasons for continental drift. Sadly, Wegener was recognized for his work after he died. Meanwhile, over three thousand years ago, the Bible correctly claimed Earth was divided.

The Bible describes the establishment of the continents (lands). The positions of the continents today, along with many other factors, allow life to thrive on this planet. Most geologists believe the continents have united and then divided on more than one occasion in Earth's history, the latest supercontinent being Pangaea, before the arrangement we observe today.

To grasp God's comments on the dividing movement of Earth's continents, it is necessary to understand Genesis 2:4 and the reference to the time frame it took for the generations of the heavens (stars). It took millions of years between the birth and death of many generations of stars. The Creator proclaims he divided Earth.

> And unto Eber were born two sons: the name of one was Peleg; for in his days was *Earth divided;* and his brother's name was Joktan. (Genesis 10:25)

In the midst of the genealogy of Noah's family, we find a reference to Earth that seems to be out of context. It seems to be a reference to a human time frame. Most of the predictions that God has made in the Bible about his creation have been hidden in the form of metaphors, parables, and dark sayings. This one is quite tricky. The chronology of Noah's family places this in a limited time if this occurred in the days (lifetime) of Peleg and his brother Joktan. Depending on the use of the word "days," which is translated from the Hebrew word *yowm*, which means "daily, ever, year, continually, always," it is, in essence, an unknown duration. In other scriptures, this word is translated as age, time, foundation, year, when, space, as long as, whole, always, ever, and evermore.

God said he formed Earth, and this took a long, long time. Then he said he divided Earth (land).

Since we understand the (day) time duration is not limited to the life of a human, and the action to which God is referring took millions of years to accomplish, we're left with Peleg. According to the Bible, the lifespan of a human during this early age of humankind was only a few hundred years at best. Observation of God's work of seafloor spreading suggests the timeframe can be millions of years. Thus, the Peleg mentioned here is not the Peleg of Noah's family, but a statement made within the record of Noah's family. Being a part of the generations of the stars of the universe, Peleg could be the name of a star that actually has a normal star lifespan of millions of years. Who has a record of the names of the stars? No one does, so this is a probable explanation.

The Creator predicted that the stars in the universe could not be numbered. Indeed, it is estimated that there are over one hundred billion galaxies that contain over one hundred billion stars *each*. How many of these names are known to humankind? If all of the names in every language ever known were applied to the stars, every name would be used up long before we finished naming the stars of the Milky Way alone. God would also have to use names not known to humankind to complete the task. So, there should have been a star named Peleg, since stars also live and die. The Creator has been confirmed correct so far about his creation. He claims to have named each and every star, but this naming of the stars cannot be confirmed on Earth.

> Lift up your eyes on high, and behold who hath created these things, That bringeth out their host by number: he *calleth them all by names* by the greatness of his might, for that he is strong in power; not one faileth. (Isaiah 40:26)

During the days of Peleg (the star), Earth was divided. The confirmed measurements by geologists of Earth's tectonic plates make it easier to estimate that the time span of the movement of the plates was quite lengthy. A man named Peleg could not have lived that long. That's not to say that Noah did not have an actual son named Peleg. Only a star could live that long.

Plate Tectonics

> Thus said God the Lord, he that created the heavens, and stretched them out; *he that spread forth Earth,* and *that which cometh out of it,* he that giveth breath unto the people upon it, and spirit to them that walk therein. (Isaiah 42:5)

This section on tectonic plates is estimated to take place during the third day or eon, within the Proterozoic Eon when the Earth's continents formed. This verse makes a series of claims about God's creative power, which includes spreading Earth itself. The English word "spread" is the Hebrew word *raqa*, which means "to beat, stamp, beat out, spread out, and stretch."

Until recently, a claim of Earth being "spread out" at any time would sound bizarre. For critics and Bible scholars alike, this verse was one of those mysteries that had no reference point until the discovery of mid-ocean spreading (thanks to Wegener in 1915).

The Bible predicts that God was spreading out Earth's surface in 700 BC, some 2,700 years ago. This is one the most important geological discoveries of all time. Earth's continents are in a state of constant change. In the middle of Earth's oceans, molten magma forces its way through the continental plates, constantly spreading them apart. This phenomenon is called seafloor spreading. The result of this heat-driven force from Earth's mantle is the constant formation of the new ocean floor and the driving of the continents. Describing the phenomenon of seafloor spreading (the primary driver of plate tectonics) is an extension of the claim of laying the foundations of the Earth, which includes the mantle. Only the Creator could have predicted the existence of seafloor spreading in the absolute darkness on the bottom of the oceans driven by the convection movement of Earth's mantle.

Science has confirmed this Iron Age claim to be correct. This is a present tense statement signifying continual spreading of the planet. No logical person would think the prophet Isaiah searched the absolute darkness of the deep ocean to make this proclamation. To date, very little of this ridge has been studied because of the inaccessibility of the totally dark, high-pressure ocean floor. This, like the other creation claims in the Bible, is the revelation from the only being who could know such things without technology: God.

The Creator controls the movement of Earth's tectonic plates, which are driven and orchestrated by the convection of Earth's mantle. There are three types of plate boundaries: convergent, divergent, and transform. Convergent boundaries are two land or ocean plate boundaries that move toward each other and collide or submerge. A transform boundary is when two tectonic plates move in opposing parallel directions while grinding against each other. A divergent boundary (also known as a constructive boundary) is where two tectonic plates move in opposite directions to each other, forcing the plates, and consequently the continents, to spread. As Earth's tectonic plates spread, magma flows out to form new ocean floor, which solidifies as it cools and continues the constant spreading of Earth. Divergent activity takes place mostly on the ocean floor.

> Seafloor spreading occurs at divergent plate boundaries. As tectonic plates slowly move away from each other, heat

Increased genera follow all ten mass extinctions

from the mantle's convection currents makes the crust more plastic and less dense. The less-dense material rises, often forming a mountain or elevated area of the seafloor.[17]

A spherical planet requires an orchestrated combination of all types of boundaries to keep it round while spreading the ocean floor. The mid-ocean ridges are wrapped around Earth like the seams of a baseball. The existence of a mountainous ridge on the ocean's floor became known earlier in the twentieth century when cable was laid across the oceans; however, the full scale of the phenomenon was discovered in the 1950s when the United States Navy used sonar to map the ocean floor. They found mountains underwater throughout all of Earth's oceans.

Due to high pressure, no person can actually go unaided to the depths of the oceans to see them firsthand. As with other predictions made by the Bible, technology had to be developed to discover the phenomenon described. For thousands of years, humans perceived we were standing on "solid ground," yet all the while, the Bible had proclaimed a moving Earth beneath our feet.

Convergent, transform, and plate boundaries are the result of divergent or mid-ocean spreading. The 1,500-mile-long Mariana Trench in the Pacific Ocean is the result of the ocean spreading and is the deepest known point on Earth, measuring seven miles deep at its lowest point. This is but one example of the Creator's ongoing geological project. The underwater volcanic activity has not only shaped the world but is also a major source of minerals needed for life in the oceans and land.

---

17   National Geographic, www.nationalgeographic.org/encyclopedia/seafloor-spreading/

To him that stretched out Earth *above the waters:* for his mercy endureth forever. (Psalm 136:6)

This verse touches on a different issue than seafloor spreading. This refers to the early stages of the splitting of the continents. The seafloor spreading in all the oceans probably started as a rift valley. The word translated as "stretched" here in Psalm 136:6 is the same Hebrew word, *raqa,* used in Isaiah 42:5, where it is translated as "to spread."

The rift valley in east Africa is a prime example of the genesis of an ocean. The first small valley on land opens until seawater enters. The spreading continues until it becomes an ocean. The east African rift has two branches, the Eastern Rift Valley and the Western Rift Valley. These valleys are edged by some of the highest mountains in Africa, Mount Kenya and Kilimanjaro. Yes, the valley is widening and the mountains are spreading apart. Given enough time, it will be an even wider waterway and possibly a sea. Who knew the mountains were moving? They are not only moving but are actually stretching apart, just as the Creator predicted. The idea of Earth moving above the waters sounds bizarre, yet it has been confirmed by observation. Let's sing that chorus one more time: science has confirmed yet another mind-blowing prediction of the Bible.

> A rift valley is a lowland region that forms where Earth's tectonic plates move apart, or rift. Rift valleys are found both on land and at the bottom of the ocean, where they are created by the process of seafloor spreading.[18]

---

18 National Geographic, www.nationalgeographic.org/encyclopedia/rift-valley/

Thus saith the LORD, thy redeemer, and he that formed thee from the womb, I am the LORD that maketh all things; that stretcheth forth the heavens alone; that *spreadeth abroad Earth by myself.* (Isaiah 44:24)

Collectively, these three verses referencing the spreading of Earth—Isaiah 42:5, 44:24, and Psalm 136:6—imply Earth is indeed millions of years old. God is saying Earth is old; it is not just the research and theories of scientists. The genesis of an ocean is referred to in Psalm 136:6. The continual process we are witnessing today in the deep oceans is referenced in Isaiah 42:5. Now in Isaiah 44:24, the word "abroad" refers to distance. Most biblical translations use "spread out" or "spread abroad." The oceans started from a rift to the size they are now. Take the rate of travel and multiply it by the current distance, and a general estimate will yield far more than six thousand years. The magnetic polarity of the North and South Poles switches from time to time. Science has verified that these changes in polarity have permanently marked the magma at the time of its hot flow. The matching parity of magnetic time durations and switching on both sides of the mid-ocean ridge is an accurate time measurement of Earth's lengthy history. However, in order for Earth to be young, the continents would have had to travel extremely fast. Travel abroad in the scripture means to travel quite some distance. The general rate of movement of the tectonic plates does not lend itself to a time reference anywhere near six thousand to ten thousand years. So, by inference, the Bible again suggests Earth is old.

Of old hast thou laid the foundation of Earth: and the heavens are the work of thy hands. (Psalm 102:25)

Through control of Earth's tectonic plates, God regulates the temperature and greenhouse gases of our planet (CH^4, CO^2, N^2O, O^3, etc.). There are seven large plates: the African, North American, South American, Eurasian, Australian, Antarctic, and Pacific plates. The Arabian, Nazca, and Philippines and others are smaller plates. Looking at a globe, one can see how the continents can be moved together to fit like a puzzle.

Pangaea began to separate about two hundred million years ago—by the hand of God, of course; as the Bible proclaims, "the work of thy hands." Consider the scripture below:

For, lo, *he that formeth the mountains*, and createth the wind, and declareth unto man what is his thought, that maketh the morning darkness, and treadeth upon the high places of Earth, The LORD, The God of hosts, is his name. (Amos 4:13)

I beheld the mountains, and, lo, they trembled, and all the hills moved lightly. (Jeremiah 4:24)

The formation of the mountains is the workmanship of the Creator through the Earth's tectonic plate movement. This is a biblical description of the cause and effect of earthquakes, which are caused by the slight movement of the land (hills). The movement of the lands is also the cause of the mountains. Again, the account of Jeremiah 4:23-28 is a demonstration of the power of the Creator to bring change at his will and for his purpose.

And God said, Let Earth bring forth grass, the herb yielding seed, and the fruit tree yielding fruit after his kind, whose seed is in itself, upon Earth: and it was so. And Earth brought forth grass, and herb yielding seed after his kind, and the tree yielding fruit, whose seed was in itself, after his kind: and God saw that it was good. And the evening and the morning were the *third day*. (Genesis 1:11–13)

The Proterozoic Eon (the third day on our biblical timeline) is when the foundation of life for all living creatures was formed. This is the beginning of the creation of plants. Later, God proclaimed creating life in abundance, starting in the water. It seems logical to prepare for the upcoming life by establishing the food supply and environment for life, particularly in the water. Plants on Earth are not limited to dry land, evident in the variety of sea grasses. Grass evidences the establishment of the foundation of the food chain for animals. The green chlorophyll of plants is the main ingredient in the process of photosynthesis, whereby the plant absorbs certain wavelengths of blue and red light of the electromagnetic spectrum and converts the light into digestible energy while reflecting green. This reflection is the green we see and is why the color green dominates plant life. The plant absorbs the blue and red light, which contain specified packets of energy, while the green light energy level is not compatible for making sugar (the "food" for plants). When a plant's leaves are brown in season, we know it likely means it's out of season for seasonal plants, and dead if it's an evergreen.

The very complex process of photosynthesis of plants is vital to all life on Earth. Oxygen is a by-product of photosynthesis, which requires these three main components to work: water, carbon dioxide, and sunlight. After the birth of our sun, the supplying of water, and the ideal atmosphere for Earth, the Creator created the complex process of photosynthesis.

According to the Bible, the creation of seed-bearing plants implies the change over time was *not* a gradual change of structure and improvement. This indicates that fertilization of the seed by another was *created*, not evolved. Fertilization is necessary for the seed to develop. Interdependence is an extremely wide crevasse to cover for Darwinian evolution. The proclamation uses the word seed four times to emphasize the structure of reproduction order that was established from the beginning of the plants. This interdependence refers to the inability to reproduce after its kind without the seed being fertilized by an opposite "gender." The interdependence of this process of fertilization and seed includes pollination, self-pollination, and cross-pollination. The same holds true for complex animal life requiring a male and female for reproduction.

The Fourth Day—Proterozoic End

> And God said, Let there be lights in the firmament of the heaven *to* divide the day from the night; and let them be *for* signs, and *for* seasons, and *for* days, and years: And let them be *for* lights in the firmament of the heaven *to* give light upon Earth: and it was so. And God made two great lights; the greater light *to* rule the day, and the lesser light *to* rule the night: he made the stars also. And God set them in the firmament of the heaven *to* give light upon Earth, And *to* rule over the day and over the night, and *to* divide the light from the darkness: and God saw that it was good. And the evening and the morning were the fourth day. (Genesis 1:14–19)

Many consider the Genesis account of the fourth day a contradiction of the account of the first day, when God created light. The first creation day description addresses the birth of our sun, the single source of all light in the solar system. The plural references to lights and "them" on the fourth day are for both the sun and moon as specific sources of light. The Hebrew word for light used in the first day is *ore*, meaning "to become light," whereas here in day four, light from the sun and moon is translated from the Hebrew word *maowr*, referring to a luminary (an archaic term meaning "a natural source of light.") The Creator further explains that the lights were created for several purposes. The eleven times the conjunctions "for" and "to" are used reflect the purposes of the two luminaries. With that in mind, the statements conclude the placement and influence of the moon and the brightness of the sun, established to properly facilitate photosynthesis among other functions, had come to fruition.

By the end of the Proterozoic Eon, Earth was producing the grass and plant life through photosynthesis as God had commanded. The duration of time is unknown for building the layers of the atmosphere and bringing them to the conditions of day four, as proclaimed in Amos 9:6.

One byproduct of photosynthesis is oxygen. Oxygen is vital for the flourishing of life to come in the Cambrian Period. This is a reference to the ability of the lights to adequately shine through the atmosphere to a greater extent, not of their creation per se.

The Creator was acknowledging the achieved goal for the length of days, seasons, and years. Scientists estimate the level of the luminosity of the sun went from 70 percent in the early Hadean Eon to about 93 percent of today's level by the end of the Precambrian Period, about 4.1 billion years. This fourth day of Genesis is the proclamation of purpose and acknowledgment of the achievement of that purpose for the sun and moon, which could be the end of the Proterozoic Eon.

Eon/Era	Day–Length	Sunlight	Moon from Earth
Hadean	7 hours	70% of today	40,000 miles
Archean	15 hours	80% of today	175,000 miles
Proterozoic	20 hours	85% of today	222,000 miles
Paleozoic	22 hours	96% of today	233,000 miles

During this lengthy biblical forth day, the actual length of days, seasons, and years changed since that of the Earth's beginning. In Earth's earliest days, scientists estimate the length of Earth's days to be about seven hours, which is similar to other early planet rotating speeds observed today by telescopes like the Kepler. Visit the Kepler Orrery animated images online to see the various orbital speeds of planets. Earth's early solar days per year are estimated to have been about 1,434.

"For signs and seasons" in Genesis 1:14~19: The lights are both the sun and moon; however, the moon is the influencer of Earth's seasons that are so critical to the life cycles of Earth's creatures. The large relative size of the moon for over three billion years has helped to keep Earth's rotation stable. Over millions of years, the Earth's rotation slowed significantly by tidal acceleration through gravitational interactions with the moon. In the Hadean Eon, the moon, with a distance of only 40,000 miles from Earth, exerted tremendous gravity on a high-speed Earth with 1,434 solar days a year. The orbital distance moved from the initial 40,000-mile distance to a distance of 222,000 miles by the end of the Proterozoic Eon.

God designed the moon to help regulate the conditions to sustain life on Earth. For example, Earth's tilt helps maintain the frozen north and south polar regions, without which the ecology of the planet would be drastically different. The continent of Antarctica, in particular, is a critical component of the deep ocean currents, which influence climate, weather, and ecosystems around the world.

> He appointed the moon for seasons: the sun knoweth his going down. (Psalm 104:19)

Obliquity refers to the axial tilt of Earth, currently at twenty-three degrees. Research suggests the long-term gravitational influence of the moon's orbit has a stabilizing effect on Earth's obliquity. The moon is also necessary to help prevent the gravitational effects of Jupiter and the sun from causing Earth's tilt to wander chaotically over a wide, climate-wrecking range.

Earth's tilt is the key to our seasons, but it has to be sustained, just as the Creator envisioned. Long before gravity and the influence of the moon was discovered or understood, the Creator proclaimed in the Bible, "The sun knoweth his going down," a reference to orbiting. How could the psalmist know of the gravitational influence the moon exerts on the four seasons that account for the cycles of life on Earth? It is undoubtedly the Creator, not the scribe who made the proclamation. The light phases of the moon that are familiar to many today also play a critical role in human activities, like the best time to plant and harvest.

> And for the precious fruits brought forth by the sun, and for the precious things put forth by the moon. (Deuteronomy 33:14)

"For day and night": It is extremely important that plant and animal life have an appropriate, regular balance of day and night. Scientists also estimate that the length of a day from its beginning formation mark of six hours per day to the end of the Proterozoic Eon to be about twenty-one hours. The number of solar days per year was reduced from an estimated 1,434 to 412 days in the Proterozoic Eon.

"To give light": The Creator made the sun and created the stars by the same lengthy process, though not at the same time. Like all stars, our sun has gone through several developmental stages. Given enough time, the sun will also die, as will all other stars in the universe. In this eon, Genesis 1:14 declares the purpose of the lights in the firmament, when, in fact, the original light source (sun) had been declared to exist at an earlier eon in Genesis 1:3-4. Earlier, God declared on day one, "Let there be light," and there was light. Before then, there was no light in our solar system.

The creation confirmation came when God "saw" the light, meaning it appeared. The luminosity was initially good enough to separate the three-hour day from the three-hour night. The light affirmed in this fourth day eon is a brighter light. Based upon the scientific model for stars, the luminosity of stars increases with age until they are in a mature state called the main sequence. When the sun was young, it was only 70 percent as bright as it is today. It seems the goal in this fourth unlabeled eon "day" of creation was to achieve adequate light upon Earth (verse seventeen). The sun came to maturity during this eon.

> As time goes on the core uses more and more of its hydrogen and contracts more and more, which makes the star brighter and brighter. At first this effect is negligible, and the one-billion-year-old sun hardly differed from the newly formed sun. But as the eons go by and hydrogen becomes less and less abundant, the rate of contraction of the core increases, it becomes brighter and brighter, and as the core increases in brightness the excess radiation flooding outward causes the rest of the star to swell to larger and larger size and greater and greater brightness itself (since it must have the same brightness as the core). As a result, the sun is now about 25% larger and 50% brighter than when first formed, and is growing about 5% larger and 10% brighter every billion years.[19]

---

19 Courtney Seligman, "The Late Main-Sequence Life of the Sun," http://cseligman.com/text/stars/sunms.htm

The time stars spend in different stages of development varies greatly. God made two "great" lights. The word "made" is translated from the Hebrew word *asah*, which means "to fashion, accomplish, or make." It is not the same word used in Genesis 1:1, "created" (*bara*), which in the context of that verse means "out of nothing." The word "great" means large in magnitude and extent, which is just what Earth needed for the abundance of life to come in the Cambrian Period. God fashioned the two great lights and the stars. In verse sixteen, the words "he made" are italicized because they were added by the translators for clarity. It is a redundant statement for the first part of the verse. He simply states that he fashioned all the lights, including the stars. However, it is the sun and the moon that rule activities on Earth. The moon reflects the sun's light, ruling the night and assisting the sun, which rules the day, giving and regulating life as the original purpose states. An assessment is made at the end (morning) of this "day." God determined that the plan had been achieved, and he called it good. The beginning of this eon could overlap earlier eons described by scientists. The biblical eons are not equivalent to the eons established by humankind. The biblical eons may not perfectly match the start/stop milestones of science. The milestone events of Genesis are subsequent to each other.

The Fifth Day—Phanerozoic Eon

Cambrian Explosion

And God said, Let the waters bring forth abundantly the moving creature that hath life, and fowl that may fly above Earth in the open firmament of heaven. And God created great whales, and every living creature that moveth, which the waters brought forth abundantly, after their kind, and every winged fowl after his kind: and God saw that it was good. And God blessed them, saying, be fruitful, and multiply, and fill the waters in the seas, and let fowl multiply in the Earth. And the evening and the morning were the fifth day. (Genesis 1:20–23)

Within the Phanerozoic Eon, the Cambrian Period marks an important point in the history of life on Earth; it is the time when more of the major groups of animals first appear in the fossil record than any other comparative period in history. This event is sometimes called the "Cambrian Explosion," because of the relatively short time over which this diversity of forms appears.[20]

The Cambrian and the Cretaceous Periods of the geological timeline span over 450 million years, which comprise the biblical fifth day. The Cambrian Period is known as the period in which a substantial diversity of complex life forms appeared. This is in concert with God's command in verse twenty for life to appear *abundantly*, not the first appearance of life in the waters. The biblical statement is also correct in its implication that this abundance of life would be concentrated in the waters. Evidence in the fossil record shows an extraordinary diversity of organisms with radically different skeletons appearing in the Cambrian Period. Animals with skeletons, bones, teeth, shells or any hard parts had not been found prior to the Cambrian. This sudden appearance of creeping things with skeletons casts some doubt on the supposed evolutionary process of gradual movement towards complexity. These creatures were created to produce after their kind as reflected by the fossil record. The precise duration of this process is unknown. The

---

20   University of California Museum of Paleontology, "The Cambrian Period," http://www.ucmp.berkeley.edu/cambrian/cambrian.php

abundance of life is a relative time duration compared to other times in which life rises after extinctions.

The total Precambrian time of about four billion years represents about seven-eighths of Earth's history; however, relatively few fossils predate the Cambrian. The "Cambrian Explosion," referred to sometimes as the "Big Bang of Life," is the relatively sudden appearance in the fossil record of most major animal body plans about five hundred forty million years ago. The pre-Cambrian Period had a limited number of small, soft-bodied animals that could not eat large particles of food. Near the end of the Proterozoic, animals were believed to be immobile and soft-bodied—no bones, shells, teeth, or other hard parts. Some soft-bodied fossils were preserved from this period, but they are few. The predominance of soft bodies is cited as the main reason for the lack of fossils before the Cambrian. However, the skeletal fossils themselves mark their own beginning through the fossil record. The Cambrian explosion got its name from the abundant life forms *in the seas* that had exoskeletons (shells), endoskeletons (bones), teeth, differentiated cells, and other hard body parts, a literal explosion of both diversities in distinct classes and abundance of life with complex bodies and internal organs. Even soft-bodied organisms, such as the four classes of sponges, appeared suddenly in the Cambrian. In this period, there is a sudden complex web of predators and prey that accompanies the animals' size, protective body parts, and the need and the ability to digest prey.

The fossil evidence of this explosion of life is not a new discovery. Charles Darwin wrote about it in his famous book *On the Origin of Species* in which he attempted to answer the big question of how this sudden array of life appeared. He asserted that, over time, other scientists would add their fossil findings to his research to get a complete picture of this event. After one hundred fifty years of additional research, the picture is indeed more complete, but it is not the picture that Darwin predicted. Darwin hypothesized a gradual progression of change leading up to the Cambrian, but the clear picture today remains one of abrupt change. Without intermediary fossils, the relatively limited time of the Cambrian and the global scale suggest these animals were created in their predatory environment, contrary to macroevolution. Macroevolution is major evolution on the scale of one species to another, in contrast to microevolution which is minor change within a species like seasonal adaptations to weather changes.

Genesis 1:20a mentions a time on Earth when the seas brought forth an abundant number of "moving" creatures. This implies that before this time, most organisms were not very mobile. The multi-continental fossil record of the Cambrian, from China to Canada to Siberia, is proof of the abundance and mobility of the Cambrian creatures. The fossils display a wide array of mobile life forms that appeared relatively suddenly in the seas. In the Cambrian and later periods, the sea was still the center of living activity. The evidence reflects the biblical account of creation and substantial growth rather than a gradual Darwinian macroevolution of growing complexity through natural selection, survival of the fittest, or mutations.

Interdependence of plant seed fertilization is a major problem for the theory of evolution before this time in Earth's history. In this context, plant or animal interdependence refers to the total dependence of a plant or animal to be fertilized by the opposite sex to reproduce. Now, the addition of animal interdependence that shows up in the Cambrian explosion is another major crevasse for evolution to cross with the addition of complex animal life requiring a male and female for reproduction. Which came first, the egg or the chicken? Observation says the chicken (rooster and hen). There is no egg without a cause, the chicken, and there is no original male or female chicken without a Creator, God. Where did God come from? Now *that* is a good question.

The same must be asked about *every* plant and animal that is fertilized. The plants were created to produce seed after its kind.

Interdependence extends beyond plants to the vital organs and components of a living creature, which make gradual macroevolution improbable. The interdependence of vital organs suggests that the heart cannot evolve without a lung to supply air, and blood is no good if the liver is not in place to filter it. Where would the heart pump the blood without a network of vessels and veins? The same applies to other vital systems of a complex creature.

Microevolution is currently observable throughout creation. Insects and bacteria change to resist pesticides we have made to kill them. Foxes and rabbits in cold regions on Earth demonstrate microevolution from the cold and warm seasons by the change of the thickness and color of their coats. However, there is simply not enough evidence of macroevolution from simplicity to complexity, from one kind of animal into another kind, to embrace it.

The reference to great whales in Genesis could refer to reptiles, which includes what has been called dinosaurs after the translation of many of the early Bibles, including the King James Bible. The Hebrew word *tannyin*, which means "dragon, serpent, sea monster, or dinosaur," is translated as "whale." Describing the whale as being great in size implies a huge animal, reflecting the stature of many of the dinosaurs. The dinosaur fossils indicate they are part of the Triassic and Jurassic Periods within this very long biblical eon.

Genesis 1:20b suggests the birds were created some undetermined time during the fifth day. Many of the birds might or might not have flown. They were created according to the Creator's wish. By observing the evidence of fossils, many of the prehistoric birds could not fly, affirming the biblical assertion of non-flying birds. The extinct dodo bird could not fly, and today, penguins fly in water but not in the air. Large birds like peacocks and chickens have limited flight capability, which is also reflected in their bone density and structure. The unique silent flight of the owl compared to the noisy hovering hummingbird is designed, not evolved. Flightless bird feather shapes can be different, and birds that don't fly usually have fewer wing bones and are missing the keel of the breastbone, the part of the bone that attaches to flight muscles. God's creation is not designed to fit our logical expectations. The fossil record shows the existence of birds that could not fly and others that could, just as the Creator declared. Not all birds were designed to fly, just as not all sharks are predators with sharp teeth.

> I beheld, and, lo, there was no man, and all the birds of the heavens were fled. (Jeremiah 4:25)

This verse of the creation account of Jeremiah is inserted here because the Creator declared there was a time in the formation of Earth in which there were birds and there was no man. God created what he chose according to his will and purpose. All of creation including mankind is subject to his time.

Mass Extinctions

The life of all creation is in the hands of the Creator. He is both the giver and taker of life. This authority has been vested in him since time immemorial. The giving of life began on an early Earth and so did the loss of life. The fossil record shows the evidence of this claim.

> The LORD killeth, and maketh alive: he bringeth down to the grave, and bringeth up. (1 Samuel 2:6)

Long before paleontologists discovered cycles of life and death in Earth's early history, the Bible affirmed the giving and taking

Increased genera follow all ten mass extinctions

of life on Earth. And the Creator, in turn, renewed life on Earth. The Creator/Sustainer declared his control of Earth's tectonic plate operation and the subsequent seafloor spreading, along with continental drift, to sculpt Earth's topography from its formation for life as it is today. In addition, he also predicts the operation of the jet stream, the rain cycle, and the deep ocean currents that sustain life on land and in the oceans. The Creator was in complete control of the ecosystem and the fate of all living creatures during Earth's early days, and he is still in control today.

> There go the ships: there is that leviathan, whom thou hast made to play therein. These wait all upon thee; that thou mayest give them their meat in due season. That thou givest them they gather: thou openest thine hand, they are filled with good. Thou hidest thy face, they are troubled: thou takest away their breath, they die, and return to their dust. Thou sendest forth thy spirit, they are created: *and thou renewest the face of Earth.* (Psalm 104:26–30)

The above scripture describes the life and death cycle along with the subsequent creation of new life over the eons. The ships are a reference to the ocean-dwelling place in which the referenced animal lives and plays. The word "leviathan" is translated from the Hebrew word *livyathan,* which means "large aquatic animal." The type of animal is not known; however, according to the scripture, it is an aquatic animal. The Creator has also declared (Genesis 1:21) to have created life in the seas, including the large sea animals, using the Hebrew word *tanniyn,* which is translated as "whales" or "dragon, serpent, or sea monster." Just as the oceanic animals today depend directly or indirectly upon the ocean currents and seasonal life cycles for sustenance, the leviathan "waits" for the life-giving cycle to come. For a time, this is the seasonal provision to which they had become accustomed. By hiding his face, the Creator's presence or provision was removed by design, and the ecosystem upon which they depended was no longer provided; their very lives (breath) were taken away, and they died and returned to the dust from which they were made.

A casual reading of these verses seems like the normal life and death cycles we witness in our lifetimes. That is, until verse thirty when the Creator sends his Spirit to create ("*bara*" in the original creation account) new life. The renewed life replaces that which has gone extinct. Furthermore, the scale of this death and renewal is the entire face of the Earth. The only death and subsequent new life on that scale is found in the fossil record. The Creator is declaring that he is the cause of the mass extinction in this and in other life and death cycles of the geological periods.

After each extinction, the Creator claimed to create life on the face of the planet. Where's the proof of the claim?

> Wherefore, when I came, was there no man? when I called, was there none to answer? Is my hand shortened at all, that it cannot redeem? or have I no power to deliver? behold, *at my rebuke I dry up the sea, I make the rivers a wilderness:* their fish stinketh, because there is no water, and dieth for thirst. (Isaiah 50:2)

The Creator makes an additional claim to have dried up the sea. Proof of drying up the sea is also proof of the first claim of turning his face from the animals. One indication is that one of the largest lakes on Earth was changed to the largest desert on Earth, an area named Wadi El Hitan, which means "whale valley." It is located in the middle of the great Sahara Desert of Egypt. Among the fossils

Increased genera follow all ten mass extinctions

found there is an abundance of five different varieties of extinct whales. Changing the sea to a desert is one way of the Creator hiding his face and making the animals go extinct. Creation is needed to replenish the Earth with different animals.

After the greatest mass extinction in history called the Permian had occurred, the Triassic period began, in which the largest land animals, the dinosaurs, appeared.

> The "age of dinosaurs" (the Mesozoic Era) included three consecutive geologic time periods (the Triassic, Jurassic, and Cretaceous Periods). Different dinosaur species lived during each of these three periods. For example, the Jurassic dinosaur *Stegosaurus* already had been extinct for approximately 80 million years before the appearance of the Cretaceous dinosaur *Tyrannosaurus*.[21]

Stegosaurus and other herbivorous dinosaurs became extinct during the Jurassic Period. The herbivorous dinosaurs were the largest dinosaurs; some weighed as much as two hundred thousand pounds. The most famous carnivorous dinosaur is the *Tyrannosaurus rex*, which appeared during the late Cretaceous Period. Many different dinosaur species appeared, lived, and went extinct at different times and geological locations.

By the end of the Cretaceous, all of the dinosaurs were extinct. Just as the Creator proclaimed, after extinction, he created new creatures to replace those that were gone. The fossil record shows he replaced the extinct creatures with more complex creatures.

---

[21] US Geological Survey, Ronald J. Litwin, Robert E. Weems, and Thomas R. Holtz, Jr., http://pubs.usgs.gov/gip/dinosaurs/together.html.

After the dinosaurs went extinct in the Cretaceous extinction, the diversity of complex mammals was created.

Darwin affirmed the emergence of more complex animals after extinctions from famine and death and attributes that emergence to natural selection and evolution. Darwin wrote:

> Thus, from the war of nature, from famine and death, the most exalted object which we are capable of conceiving, namely, the production of the higher animals, directly follows.[22]

More complex animals were indeed *created* after each extinction event. The scriptures predicted extinction and the subsequent renewal of life on Earth. It is extremely difficult to cause an Earth-wide terrestrial and marine life extinction. It is equally difficult for an Earth-wide diversity of species to follow a mass reduction in both life and species. The Bible told of this unlikely phenomenon of death and increased life before fossils were recognized as originating in prehistoric times.

The Creator brought into existence the sudden flourishing of life. The graph below affirms exactly what the Creator told in the Bible.[23] Biodiversity increases immediately after both the five minor and five major extinction events, because a new creation event follows. That's ten for ten.

---

22 Charles Darwin, *On the Origin of Species, Sixth Edition*. (London: John Murray, 1859).
23 "Biodiversity during the Phanerozoic," *Wikimedia Commons*, https://commons.wikimedia.org/wiki/File:Phanerozoic_Biodiversity.svg.

Increased genera follow all ten mass extinctions

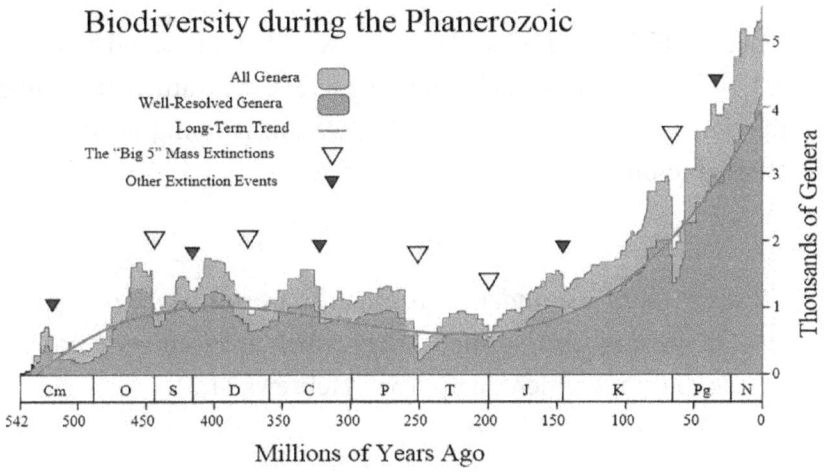

The greatest extinction of sea life and terrestrial life occurred during the most severe extinction event in history: the end of the Permian, where 90 percent of all marine and terrestrial species were lost. However, the principle of extinction and the subsequent abundance of diverse life are shown in the fossil record. Second to the Permian extinction in severity is the K/T extinction, which was the last and most famous of the five major extinctions, because it was the one that killed the last dinosaurs and 50 percent of all other species. The absolute extinction of *all* dinosaurs occurred across the then-separated continents of the entire planet, while many other species, such as environmentally sensitive frogs, survived, making it difficult to determine the cause or causes of the cataclysm.

The Creator controls the entire ecosystem and must have decided once again to institute his own life reset button. One logical question: Could humans live with huge, carnivorous dinosaurs when humans would obviously be prey? Both could not live together on the planet, so the Creator removed one to establish the other.

It is no accident that all dinosaurs are extinct. Every time man creates a more complex instrument, it requires more complex information or instruction to make and operate the increased complexity. This is also true with the Creator: an increase in the complexity of living creatures required increased information and instruction. Hebrews 11:3 declares the "worlds," translated from the Greek work *aion*, meaning "different ages," were framed according to the word (information) of God. Creation is doing what it was instructed to do.

> *Through faith we understand that the worlds were framed by the word of God*, so that things which are seen were not made of things which do appear. (Hebrews 11:3)

Below are descriptions of the five great extinction events; however, other minor events occurred throughout history. After extinctions, Darwinian evolutionists suggest ecological niches just opened up and other species took advantage of the opportunity. The question is, how did those advanced species come about to fill the niche? Following extinction, more diverse, higher, and more complex creatures came into existence. The God of the Bible predicted the life, death, and new life cycles that the fossil record reflects, as well as a diversification of species. With 99.9 percent of all species being extinct, "survival of the fittest" did not exactly allow them to survive.

> Extinction is the complete demise of a species. It takes place when *all* individuals of a species die out. Extinction has occurred throughout the history of life on Earth. It is the ultimate fate of all species. In fact, it has been estimated that 99.9% of all species that have ever lived on Earth are now extinct.[24]

---

24 "Extinction," *paleobiology.si.edu*, http://paleobiology.si.edu/geotime/main/foundation_life4.html.

Increased genera follow all ten mass extinctions

Ordovician-Silurian extinction, global extinction event occurring during the Hirnantian Age (445.6 million to 443.7 million years ago) of the Ordovician Period and the subsequent Rhuddinian Age (443.7 million to 439 million years ago) of Silurian Period that an estimated 85 percent of all Ordovician species.[25]

The Devonian Extinction. Toward the end of the Devonian, nearly 70% of all invertebrate species vanished during the Late Devonian extinction. Marine species (especially tropical ones) suffered the most extinctions, followed by freshwater species, whereas terrestrial species were hardly affected.[26]

The end-Permian extinction occurred 252.2 million years ago, decimating 90 percent of marine and terrestrial species, from snails and small crustaceans to early forms of lizards and amphibians. "The Great Dying," as it's now known, was the most severe mass extinction in Earth's history, and is probably the closest life has come to being completely extinguished.[27]

The Triassic–Jurassic extinction event marks the boundary between the Triassic and Jurassic periods, 201.3 million years ago, and is one of the major extinction events of the Phanerozoic eon, profoundly affecting life on land and in the oceans.[28]

---

[25] "Ordovician Silurian extinction," *Britannica.com*, http://www.britannica.com/EBchecked/topic/1523112/Ordovician-Silurian-extinction.
[26] "The Devonian," *paleobiology.si.edu*, http://paleobiology.si.edu/geotime/main/devonian4.html.
[27] Jennifer Chu, "Mass extinction," *MIT*, http://web.mit.edu/newsoffice/2011/mass-extinction-1118.html.
[28] "Triassic-Jurassic extinction event," *Wikipedia*, http://en.wikipedia.org/wiki/Triassic-Jurassic_extinction_event.

Perhaps the most notable event of the Cretaceous was its conclusion. About 65 million years ago the second greatest mass extinction in Earth history occurred, resulting in the loss of the dinosaurs as well as nearly 50% of all species.[29]

The Sixth Day—The Cenozoic Era

And God said, Let Earth bring forth the living creature after his kind, cattle, and creeping thing, and beast of Earth after his kind: and it was so. And God made the beast of Earth after his kind, and cattle after their kind, and everything that creepeth upon Earth after his kind: and God saw that it was good. (Genesis 1:24–25)

Following the extinction of all dinosaurs during the Cretaceous Period about sixty-five million years ago, the current geological era, the Cenozoic, began. Here, the Bible explains, terrestrial animals, such as mammals and other complex creatures, were created after the predicted extinction and restoration cycles of created life instituted by the Creator (Psalm 104:26–30). After the Mesozoic era came the Cenozoic Era, in which many new creatures appeared, including mammals, new species of birds, and creeping things. As predicted by the Bible, new life follows the extinction events. The Ediacaran extinction preceded the Cambrian explosion. The K-Pg (also known as K-T) extinction, which is one of the five major global extinction events in history affecting both land and water life, preceded the Cenozoic Era. The word "Cenozoic" is a Greek term meaning "new life" and is the shortest geological era, lasting only

---

[29] "The Cretaceous," *paleobiology.si.edu*, http://paleobioloby.si.edu/geotime/main/htmlversion/cretaceous4.html.

sixty-six million years. The dinosaurs went extinct at this event. The Creator declared living creatures were brought forth after their kind. The Cenozoic is considered the age of the mammals. In addition, significant numbers of other species, including insects, reptiles, birds, and fish, appeared upon the scene. What happened to the dinosaurs in the different eons and subsequent extinction when different species arose after each of the extinctions? The same extinctions that killed the dinosaurs allowed many frogs to survive.

The word "cattle" in Genesis 1:24 refers to herbivorous animals capable of domestication and labor. Some are "dumb" or non-intelligent creatures. Creeping things refer to any animal that is mobile, including, but not limited to, insects. The beasts of Earth include the wild, ravenous, and other creatures. The domesticated and wild animals are the two types of the various mammals created after their kind, as indicated by the fossil record. God's "days" or eons do not have the same duration, and some can overlap one another compared to those established by researchers. This is God's sixth marked period from the beginning of the solar system. Once again, God renewed the face of the planet with new creations after the extinction of the dinosaurs. The new creations after extinctions are a biblical answer to how new creatures came into being. Everything is made from the dirt of the ground and, upon death, returns to the ground.

The diversity of insects increased dramatically along with the increase of flowering plants that occurred in the Cretaceous. After the K-T mass extinction, an estimated 75 percent of all species, including insects, disappeared. Entomologists estimate insects account for 80 percent of all animal species during this period. The Creator mentioned the creeping things because they are important to the food chain of other animals. After the extinctions, they needed to be replenished (new genera were created). Genera are a major subdivision of a family or subfamily in the classification of organisms, usually consisting of more than one species. This is not a reference to the original creation of insects.

> And God said, Let us make man in our image, after our likeness: and let them have dominion over the fish of the sea, and over the fowl of the air, and over the cattle, and over all Earth, and over every creeping thing that creepeth upon Earth. So God created man in his own image, in the image of God created he him; male and female created he them. (Genesis 1:26–27)

The word "God" here in verse twenty-six, and throughout the creation account of Genesis, is the Hebrew word *Elohiym*. It is the plural form of the singular Hebrew word *Elowahh*, which means "God." This is the reason for the use of "us" in the declaration to make humankind. Thus, we have the triune God: God the Father, God the Son, and God the Holy Spirit, three in one. Humans were created body, soul, and spirit in the likeness of the triune God.

This threeinone concept has been a stumbling block for many when it comes to comprehending this aspect of God. To better understand it, let's go to Paul's first epistle to the Corinthians. It reveals the operation of God the Father, Son, and Holy Ghost, which we call "the Godhead." I will use a construction hierarchy as a metaphor to explain the Godhead's operation, from the eternal past up to now. It's kind of hidden, being written in reverse order, starting with verse six, to verse five, and then to four.

> Now there are diversities of gifts, but the same Spirit. And there are differences of administrations, but the same Lord.

Increased genera follow all ten mass extinctions

> And there are diversities of operations, but it is the same God which worketh all in all. (1 Corinthians 12:4-6)

Verse six refers to God as working all in all. Verse five refers to the Lord (Jesus) having the administration. Verse four refers to the Holy Spirit, who operates the end working (gifts). In a large construction project, the architect is the one who draws up the plans for the project. God is the architect. He designed everything about this project, down to the smallest detail. Now that we have a master plan, we need a general contractor to execute the plan. Jesus is the general contractor, and the architect's detailed plans are administered and executed through him. He is the authority on the project. Now that we have a general contractor, we need craftsmen. The craftsmen are the ones who execute the work on the spot through their varied talents (gifts). The gifts come through the Holy Spirit.

With these gifts, the craftsmen perform the work according to the detailed plans of the architect under the authority of the general contractor. Upon project completion, the architect can rightfully say that he built the project and that every aspect is his idea. The general contractor can rightfully say that he built the project and administered every aspect of the plans. The craftsmen can rightfully say they built the project, executing every aspect of the plans. The architect, general contractor, and the craftsmen operate as one to execute the project.

The same is true of God, Jesus, and the Holy Spirit in the creation of the universe. Remove any one of them, and the project would not have been completed. When God said, "Let us make," we understand that all three members of the Godhead were involved. This entire creative and sustaining operation includes Jesus as outlined in Colossians 1:15–20. Jesus was there from the beginning executing his authority in the creation of the universe and humankind. The

Holy Spirit was there to execute God's commands, as he did in the first era of the formation of Earth, as stated in Genesis 1:2. All creation is by the triune God.

After the creation of the various animals, plants, insects and the environment, the stage was set for humankind. The decision was made to fashion humankind. This is not an alteration of another creature. Humans are made from the dirt of Earth, just as Earth was formed from previous materials made by the stars. This was part of a master plan to get the material needed to make the Earth then create humans and animals. Made in the image of *Elohim*, man is the natural alpha creature, three in one: body, soul, and spirit. The extent of the detail of God's image, silhouette, and composition are not known. However, descriptions of visions God showed to humans indicate some resemblance to the Ancient of Days (God) in the Book of Daniel and to Jesus, the Son of God, in the Book of Revelation.

> I beheld till the thrones were cast down, and the Ancient of days did sit, whose garment was white as snow, and the hair of his head like the pure wool: his throne was like the fiery flame, and his wheels as burning fire. (Daniel 7:9)

> And in the midst of the seven candlesticks one like unto the Son of man, clothed with a garment down to the foot, and girt about the paps with a golden girdle. His head and his hairs were white like wool, as white as snow; and his eyes were as a flame of fire; And his feet like unto fine brass, as if they burned in a furnace; and his voice as the sound of many waters. And he had in his right hand seven stars: and out of his mouth went a sharp two-edged sword: and his countenance was as the sun shineth in his strength. (Revelation 1:13–16)

These two verses offer a limited comparison of humankind with the Creator. However, God describes Adam and his son using the same wording, which suggests a similitude. Not only will the creation produce of its kind, but a child is expected to resemble his father and mother in a way that is distinct from other humans. This makes humans even more special to the Creator, who is also considered our Father. This is also contrary to the atheist, who suggests that humankind is not special, existing purely by chance in a far corner of the enormous universe.

> And Adam lived a hundred and thirty years, and begat a son in his own likeness, after his image; and called his name Seth. (Genesis 5:3)

All creatures, including Neanderthals, *Homo erectus*, and all other primates, were created by the God of the Bible. There is one God, one Creator. However, these creatures were simple, non-intelligent beings. The biblical human created from the ground is the ultimate intellectual, being able to communicate in a variety of languages. Today, about sixty-five hundred different languages are spoken on Earth. Humans are fully capable of identifying animals and assigning characteristic names to each of them. In the likeness of their Creator, humans are able to design and build using materials supplied by the Creator. We observe and learn the laws of nature that guide the vast and complicated universe. Humans can create motor vehicles to carry us about and do work for us. Although not designed to fly like a bird, we have created flying machines to make any bird jealous. No other creature is able to accomplish anything close to humans.

Compared to all other creatures on Earth, humans are limited in their physical strength, speed, camouflage, protection, paws, teeth, and so forth, yet humankind dominates every other creature, as God commanded. In the image of God's intellect, humankind's domination is via our intellect. No creature is capable of rising up to subvert our status.

> And the LORD God formed man of the dust of the ground, and breathed into his nostrils the breath of life; and man became a living soul. (Genesis 2:7)

The word "dust" of Genesis 2:7 is the Hebrew word *aphar*, which means "ore, powder from the ground." The word "ground" is translated from the Hebrew word *adamah*, which means "the land." The dust is small particles of the ground. The sum of the minerals needed to create a human required an extensive gathering of those minerals from various locations. The concept of the composition of humankind coming from the dirt points to the source of the chemicals that the Creator used. God used these fifty-nine elements found in the planet's crust to construct the complex human cells, including DNA, and added life. According to evolution, natural selection without any volition has taken the fifty-nine elements mentioned along with their various percentages and created the humans we see today. The odds of this happening by accident are beyond astronomical, even over an unfathomably long timeline. God created and gave humans life just as he had done for all other creatures in ages past.

DNA has revolutionized the criminal justice system and is now used to overturn many false convictions that were based upon older, less accurate identification methods. The new technology of DNA evidence has also had an impact in the case of history, which shows the Neanderthals and Denisovans are different creatures and thus a different and earlier creation of God. Antiquated methods

Increased genera follow all ten mass extinctions

of using similarities in skin and hair to determine an ancestor are, well, antiquated.

> A second mtDNA sequence, announced in 2000, was derived from a 29,000 year old Neanderthal found in Mezmaiskaya Cave, Russia (Ovchinnikov et al. 2000). Although the Mezmaiskaya Cave sequence was slightly different than the Feldhofer Neanderthal, the two Neanderthal mtDNA sequences were distinct from those of modern humans. These results confirmed the earlier findings that showed that Neanderthals were unlikely to have contributed to the modern human genome.[30]

Horses and donkeys are crossbred to produce mules. A limited number of another species can crossbreed; however, they did not evolve one from the other.

The spin doctors have really put the "spin" on the DNA numbers when comparing humans to other animals to present a quantitative similarity between creatures to support a Darwinian evolutionary theory. The function of DNA and percentages shared in common between species can be deceiving. Humans and cats share 90 percent of their DNA. A cow has 80 percent, a mouse has 75 percent, a fruit fly 60 percent, and a banana 50 percent of our DNA. What does that really say? Does 50 percent commonality represent 50 percent of knowledge, resemblance, lifespan, or complexity? Are bananas "50 percent like" humans?

---

[30] "Neanderthal mitochondrial DNA," *Smithsonian Museum of Natural History*, http://humanorigins.si.edu/evidence/genetics/ancient-dna-and-neanderthals/neanderthal-mitochondrial-dna.

None of these have any bearing on the comparison between a banana and a human being. All life has fundamental functions given to them by the Creator and made from Earth's minerals. Since creatures are made from the same source, use the same food sources, and possess the same metabolic functions to live in the same environment, there should be expectations of genetic similarities.

Hence, comparing percentages of DNA overlap is not a good representation of similarity. A case in point: cystic fibrosis is one of the most common, fatal genetic diseases in the United States. The defective gene was discovered in 1989, and a cure or method to correct the disorder of the defective gene has yet to be discovered. This single gene is one out of the estimated twenty-eight thousand genes in humans, so having the disease means only a .00004 percent error in the code. This shows the dramatic impact a very small deviation in the DNA structure can cause.

The genetic difference *between* humans is 0.1 percent on average. From that 0.1 percent come all the differences that make us individuals: race, hair, facial features, body type, fingerprints, and our DNA "fingerprint," which is accurate enough to qualify as criminal evidence for individuality. Look around and observe the many differences in all humans that reflect only a 0.1 percent difference in the genome.

When a proposed 4 percent difference between humans and primates is cited as evidence of Darwinian macroevolution, what is overlooked is the mountain of difference in the genome. Even the 4 percent difference is not the complete story because the entire genome of the primate and the human is *not* used, only select parts. And that depends upon the various ways in which it can be calculated. The total genetic differences, not select parts between humans and other creatures, are what make for different species or what the Bible terms "kinds." Below are a few more details that need to be considered concerning purported differences. The data can be

Increased genera follow all ten mass extinctions

interrogated until it says what the interrogator wants to hear. The trimmed down data is then presented in the comparisons.

> For about 23% of our genome, we share no immediate genetic ancestry with our closest living relative, the chimpanzee. This encompasses genes and exons to the same extent as intergenic regions.[31]

> Despite the many similarities found between human and chimp genomes, the researchers emphasized that important differences exist between the two species. About 35 million DNA base pairs differ between the shared portions of the two genomes, each of which, like most mammalian genomes, contains about 3 billion base pairs. In addition, there are another 5 million sites that differ because of an insertion or deletion in one of the lineages, along with a much smaller number of chromosomal rearrangements.[32]

And the LORD God said, it is not good that the man should be alone; I will make him a help meet for him. And out of the ground the LORD God formed every beast of the field, and every fowl of the air; and brought them unto Adam to see what he would call them: and whatsoever Adam called every living creature, that was the name thereof. And Adam gave names to all cattle, and to the fowl of the air, and to every beast of the field; but for Adam there was not found a help meet for him. And the LORD God caused a deep sleep to fall upon Adam, and he slept: and he took one of his ribs,

---

31   Ingo Ebersberger, Petra Galgoczy, et al., "Mapping Human Genetic Ancestry," *Molecular Biology and Evolution*, Vol. 24 (10); 2266-2276.
32   National Genome Research Institute, "New Genome Comparison Finds Chimps, Humans, Very Similar at the DNA Level," *genome.gov*, http://www.genome.gov/15515096.

and closed up the flesh instead thereof; And the rib, which the LORD God had taken from man, made he a woman, and brought her unto the man. And Adam said, This is now bone of my bones, and flesh of my flesh: she shall be called Woman, because she was taken out of Man. (Genesis 2:18–23)

God created all the animals from the minerals of the ground just like he created humankind. The fact that the source of life material and the method of creating life is the same for humans and for the animals explains the similarities found in the DNA. These verses are a summary of previous work that God accomplished, creating the animals, preparing a designated garden for Adam, and the time to bring all those animals to be identified and named. Adam, the intellectual leader of Earth, was not a hunter-gatherer in the sense of the caveman. Intellect eluded all earlier creatures; however, humans were created with a high intellect, reflecting the image of their Creator. Adam had no means of reproducing himself without Eve. God declared the obvious: Adam needed help to accomplish the reproduction of humans.

This first major operation on a human was performed on Adam by the Creator. As in the process of surgery today, God put Adam in a state in which he would not feel or know what was happening during his surgery. The creation of Eve was unique. She was not born of a woman and not created directly from the ground. This is an example of how humans cannot merely look at how the Creator has done things in the past and, in turn, conclude it is the only way he can do it. To this day, women and men are quite different creatures, even though they are of the same species. "Men are from Mars, and women are from Venus," as the saying goes. Marriage is not intended to be a union of sameness, but a formula for life. The context of Jesus's answer to the Pharisees concerns divorce in Mark

10:3-9; the original purpose at the beginning of the creation of male and female in day six is to be married.

> But from the beginning of the creation God made them male and female. For this cause shall a man leave his father and mother, and cleave to his wife; And they twain shall be one flesh: so then they are no more twain, but one flesh. (Mark 10:6–8)

God created them male and female with all that was needed to reproduce after its kind. Each sexually reproducing mate is independently vital to the life-giving genome necessary for the continuation of the creation. Single-celled asexual organisms simply duplicate themselves by dividing and making an exact genetic copy of themselves without genetic variation and, therefore, both organisms share the same genetic weaknesses. For asexual single-celled organisms, if the environment changes, the consequences could be deadly to every individual. Scientists hypothesize this is what drives evolution. But how can an asexual, single-celled organism become anything other than itself when it can only reproduce an exact copy of itself? How can it become a multicellular organism with specialized cells by producing exact genetic copies with no genetic variation?

For a Creator who expands the universe, the creation of a human is not a real challenge. God created sexual, multicellular creatures with a mate to supply the connecting genome coding for complex life, both male and female—not just for humans, but for all sexual organisms, including plants.

Adam and Eve

> And hath made of one blood all nations of men for to dwell on all the face of Earth. (Acts 17:26a)

Despite the outward appearance of the different races, even in biblical days, God stated that all humans share the same blood. Austrian scientist Karl Landsteiner of the University of Vienna discovered human blood typing in 1900. This declaration goes further than blood. It is a well-known fact that a mother and her baby can have different blood types. The Bible says that all humans have the same father, Adam, and the same mother, Eve. Adam and Eve were modern humans with no biological antecedents. Extraordinary claims require extraordinary evidence. Once again, upon examination of the science, we find the Bible is correct regarding the beginning of the universe, the expanding universe, the accelerating universe, the flat universe, and so on. The discovery of DNA was alleged to unveil the workings of natural selection in favor of macroevolution. The evidence has certainly unveiled the truth; that is, of the Bible.

National Geographic and IBM launched a global genetic search to find the father of all humans entitled "The Search for Adam." This and other scientific studies did not reveal what many expected from genetics. Many believed science would prove the Bible wrong in one of the Bible's most popular affirmations, but the science indicates every human came from the same father. The facts suggest male Y chromosome genetics came from a single man, dubbed "Scientific Adam," who is the father of every human alive. The National Geographic documentary about the project suggests it is not the Adam of the Bible, but the God of the Bible predicted all humans have one father. Interestingly, the Hebrew word "Adam" in the book of Genesis is a plural name that means "humankind or people."

Increased genera follow all ten mass extinctions

The study of mitochondrial DNA genetics that is passed down from mother to daughter suggests a single woman as the mother of all humans, called "Mitochondrial Eve." Once again, the God of the Bible contends that all humans have one mother. While the intellectual Adam was naming the things of nature, he named his wife "Eve," which means "the mother of all living" (Genesis 3:20).

Scientific studies suggest that both scientific Adam and Eve lived in east Africa. The famous and mysterious Garden of Eden is said by the Bible to be located in east Africa, Ethiopia in particular. In biblical times, it had one river that flowed out of it that separated into four branches—like the river Gihon flowed in Ethiopia. Surprise!

> And the name of the second river is Gihon: the same is it that compasseth the whole land of Ethiopia. And the name of the third river is Hiddekel: that is it which goeth toward the east of Assyria. And the fourth river is Euphrates. And the LORD God took the man, and put him into the garden of Eden to dress it and to keep it. (Genesis 2:13-15)

It just so happens to be a match to the recent African origin model of human origination and migration. There is also a multiregional origin model of humans that suggests humans evolved from many regions of Earth. However, Mitochondrial Eve's genetic results do not lend themselves to the multiregional macroevolution model, which requires interbreeding between humans and other creatures.

The scientific community as a whole does not embrace Scientific Adam and Mitochondrial Eve as the same individuals spoken of in the Bible as the first man and woman. That would bury the theory of the macroevolution of humankind. The genetic evidence speaks of one father and one mother. A "bottleneck population theory" attempts to answer the Scientific Adam and Mitochondrial Eve question.

This theory suggests humans descended from a small population of various breeding pairs living in a general area. Furthermore, due to numerous adverse environmental conditions, over time the population of humans was reduced to small populations called "the bottleneck."

For the bottleneck theory to work, this bottleneck of humans should have contained thousands of humans; however, according to the theory, only one each of scientific Adam and Eve's genetic line survived. As the bottleneck implies, there must have been a larger population in time before scientific Adam and Eve. Not only did one of Adam and one of Eve's seed survive, but by chance, all of the descendants of all the other humans were wiped out. This seems to be an extreme case of complexity driven by chance.

The bottleneck hypothesis is similar to the cosmic multiverse hypothesis in that there is no real evidence for it and there appears to be no method of obtaining evidence. It proposes the existence of tens of thousands of humans who disappeared without a genetic trace, allowing only scientific Adam and Eve to be the father and mother of all. However, the genetic evidence suggests there were one father and one mother for all humans, as the biblical account proclaims.

The working assumption is that macroevolution happened, and everything around it has to be formed to accommodate that framework. The population bottleneck estimate is just that, an estimate. There are variables that are part of the method of calculating this bottleneck population. These variables include the window of fertility for males and/or females, which is unknown. The duration of generations is also unknown, as are life spans. Mating characteristics, such as the ratio of men to women or the rate of survival of the offspring are not known. Therefore, what parameters are to be used when calculating the population dynamics when vital data about the ancients is not available? When the range of existence for Scientific Adam is estimated to be from 50,000 to 338,000 years ago, clearly, the

Increased genera follow all ten mass extinctions

estimate is extremely speculative. With these unknowns, the time of Adam cannot be affirmed and certainly cannot confirm Adam and Eve did not live at the same time. How could scientific Adam and Eve both be the father and mother of all humans and *not* live at the same time and in the same place?

> And God blessed them, and God said unto them, Be fruitful, and multiply, and replenish Earth, and subdue it: and have dominion over the fish of the sea, and over the fowl of the air, and over every living thing that moveth upon Earth. And God said, Behold, I have given you every herb bearing seed, which is upon the face of all Earth, and every tree, in the which is the fruit of a tree yielding seed; to you it shall be for meat. (Genesis 1:28–29)

> And to every beast of Earth, and to every fowl of the air, and to everything that creepeth upon Earth, wherein there is life, I have given every green herb for meat: and it was so. And God saw everything that he had made, and, behold, it was very good. And the evening and the morning were the sixth day. (Genesis 1:30–31)

God's newest and highest natural creation was granted dominion over all creatures and Earth. Then God blessed the couple with the promise of provisions for them and their subjects. God introduced himself as the sustainer of all life on Earth. Adam and Eve were to do their part by tending, and God would provide the plants of Earth as a base food for all land-based animals. The same held true for the base food plankton for all ocean-dwelling animals. Here, the omission of animal meat that could be used for food does not mean that meat was not meant to be consumed. As a matter of fact,

God declares that his original purpose for the creation of animals before Adam was in part for food. The Bible declares in the book of Timothy that meat was created with the purpose to be eaten and to be considered good at creation.

> Forbidding to marry, and commanding to abstain from meats, which *God hath created to be received* with thanksgiving of them which believe and know the truth. For every creature of God is *good*, and nothing to be refused, if it be received with thanksgiving: (1Timothy 4:3-4)

Animals were created in previous periods before man were carnivores, as the fossil evidence of their teeth and digestive systems shows. A case in point is the dinosaurs, many of which were carnivores. Those who argue for the existence of a vegetarian diet before the fall do not address the food of the fish. Ocean animals are almost all carnivores. This implies the Earth is millions and even billions of years old. Those who believe an old Earth violates the scriptures because thorns found in the fossil record is in contrast with Genesis 3:17–19a, based on Adam being created less than ten thousand years ago and subsequently fell into sin and cursed. Based upon that assumption, the thorn fossil record must be the approximate age of Adam.

> And unto Adam he said, because thou hast hearkened unto the voice of thy wife, and hast eaten of the tree, of which I commanded thee, saying, thou shalt not eat of it: cursed is the ground for thy sake; in sorrow shalt thou eat of it all the days of thy life; Thorns also and thistles shall it bring forth

to thee; and thou shalt eat the herb of the field; In the sweat of thy face shalt thou eat bread. (Genesis 3:17-19a)

The curse for both Eve and Adam seems to be an addition to what was already established before the fall. For Eve, her sorrows would be multiplied or added. However, anything multiplied by zero is zero. The ground is certainly cursed. The phrase 'to thee' at the end of that command leaves the door open that thorns were already growing somewhere. However, without that phrase, the command would be an absolute statement of the creation of thorns. Is it really saying that Adam was not capable of sweating?

The curse is more than simply thorns, thistles, and sweat. If that is the literal limit, it is directed only to farmers and has been overcome by modern technology by the use of herbicides in their fields. Any modern farm has no thorns, grass, or weed in their plantings. The same holds true with the reference to sweating to make a living. Those who live in cold regions of Earth or work in air-conditioned spaces have also negated God's curse of the sweat of the brow.

Both curse references are idioms that represent a much broader, unavoidable curse upon the scope of life on Earth, from all types of everyday work to childbirth. The thorns figuratively represent difficulty and pain intertwined in all forms of endeavors humans set out to achieve. Childbirth is not only struggle and pain at the birth, but *also* continual struggle and pain in raising the children to adulthood. The struggle in our human relationships. All forms of work are plagued with problems of all sorts. The difficulty is so prevalent we have bestowed upon it the name of "Murphy's Law"— in the process of doing something, what can go wrong, will. This also includes all the types of entropies explained in this book.

Concluding the sixth day, Genesis 1:31 is a summary statement by the Creator concerning all his natural creation. God saw or observed *everything* he made. From first second of creation to the completion of Earth and the formation of man, all were declared to be exceedingly good. The Creator was satisfied with his work.

The Seventh Day

> Thus the heavens and Earth were finished, and all the host of them. And on the seventh day God ended his work which he had made; and he rested on the seventh day from all his work which he had made. (Genesis 2:1–2)

Verse one is a concluding statement wrapping up the entire seven-day account, starting with the word "thus." The referenced time spans, from the start of creation to the advent of humankind, are contained in Genesis 1:1–31. The phrase "all the host of them" refers to all of the galaxies, clusters, planets and stars that make up the universe. The word "finished" does not signify an absolute completion. This Hebrew word means "to accomplish and cease," which corresponds to the fact God rested at a milestone point, but he had not retired. After nearly fourteen billion years, the Creator declared a time to pause or rest from his work. It seems as if the creation of humankind was a milestone for the Creator—not the only milestone but a milestone for sure. After four billion years, the crowning creation was that of humankind. God declared this an eon or period of rest from his work. But his work as sustainer is still active.

> For in six days the LORD made heaven and Earth, the sea, and all that in them is, and rested the seventh day: wherefore the LORD blessed the sabbath day, and hallowed it. (Exodus 20:11)

Increased genera follow all ten mass extinctions

This sabbath sign that was to be exercised in Old Testament times pointed to the real sabbath of man found in Hebrews 4:8-11. Here, the scriptures compare God's rest after the work of creation to our rest after lifelong work for him. Our greatest rest is when we cease from our works as God did from his. This is the real sabbath rest, not a sign. Even this rest is not absolute.

> For if Jesus had given them rest, then would he not afterward have spoken of another day. There remaineth therefore a rest to the people of God. For he that is entered into his rest, he also hath ceased from his own works, as God did from his. Let us labour therefore to enter into that rest, lest any man fall after the same example of unbelief. (Hebrews 4:8-11)

Genesis 2:4-6 is a summary of the previous work from the original creation of the universe to the creation of mankind. As stated earlier, the generations of the heavens and Earth signify the life and death of the stars, which is the time frame (in the day or eon) that he made these things. The Earth was made during the early solar system. The plants and herbs of the field were created after the rain cycle was established.

> These are the generations of the heavens and of the Earth when they were created, in the day that the LORD God made the Earth and the heavens, And every plant of the field before it was in the Earth, and every herb of the field before it grew: for the LORD God had not caused it to rain upon the Earth, and there was not a man to till the ground. But there went up a mist from the Earth, and watered the whole face of the ground. (Genesis 2:4-6)

The second chapter of Genesis continues with references to the conditions and requirements presented to Adam before his sinful fall from his relationship with his Creator. Verse fifteen establishes the garden required work to maintain it. Verse sixteen establishes Adam's need for food. Some believe Adam was created to live forever, but does an eternal being require food? What would happen to Adam if he did not eat? The very process of digestion requires entropy to obtain energy from the food. All food, whether plant or flesh, must have recently lived for it to have any nutritional value. Adam's food before the fall needed to have nutritional value from recent life to sustain him. Also before the fall, did all the fish eat grass, fruit, or meat?

Life can only be sustained by life. Verse nine reveals a mysterious tree containing the most unusual fruit, the tree of life. A distinction must be made between the life from the plants and life from this special tree. Eating the fruit from the tree of life would yield a life with no natural death, before or after the fall. This is affirmed by the Bible in Genesis chapter three where God drove Adam out of the garden because of the tree of life, and placing a guard to prevent access to the tree of life, so Adam could not take his natural hand and eat of the tree and live forever. Before the fall, access was given to Adam and Eve to the tree of life to live forever if they ate of it; without it, they were created to die just as the stars, Earth, and every natural thing in this universe.

The fall of Adam could only affect the jurisdiction of Earth because the universe was never under the jurisdiction of Adam. Adam was given limited dominion on the Earth in which he had access and could affect; in addition, his Earth dominion does not go back in time before his arrival. The Bible declares there is death beyond Adam's jurisdiction, which could not be affected by his fall because the heavens have been dying before the creation of the Earth. In the scripture below God declares those who dwell on the Earth shall die in like manner as the heavens.

Increased genera follow all ten mass extinctions

> Lift up your eyes to the heavens, and look upon the Earth beneath: for the heavens shall vanish away like smoke, and the Earth shall wax old like a garment, and *they that dwell therein shall die in like manner*: (Isaiah 51:6)

The first death Adam experienced was a spiritual death. He caused all his descendants to be separated from God. As stated in Romans chapter five, by one man sin entered into the world and death by sin: and by Jesus's death, death was conquered. Jesus died in our stead that we should never die.

So, if Jesus died in our stead, why do 100 percent of all Christians eventually die? In John 11:26, Jesus said we should never experience death if we believe in him. The death he referred is a spiritual death or separation from our Creator, as happened to Adam when he sinned. By his death Jesus restored that relationship which is life, thus we should not be separated from God again, even when we die a natural death. If the death that Jesus conquered is our natural death, Jesus did not accomplish his mission because we all are yet dying. Natural death before the fall does not affect the work of the cross. The work of the cross saves us from spiritual death.

> Jesus said unto her, I am the resurrection, and the life: he that believeth in me, though he were dead, yet shall he live: And whosoever *liveth and believeth in me shall never die.* Believest thou this? (John 11:25-26)

We are still in the seventh day just like we are still in the vision of Daniel (8:26). The duration of both days is unknown. The Creator has proclaimed his period of rest. However, it only relates to the initial act of creating, because the complex and vast universe requires a *sustainer*. Revelation 4:11 speaks of creation in both the present and past tense. Thus, the seventh day of creation has not ended. In the seventh day, the focus changes from Creator to Sustainer.

> Thou art worthy, O Lord, to receive glory and honour and power: for thou hast created all things, and for thy pleasure they *are and were* created. (Revelations 4:11)

Chapter 5

Sustainer

Thou, even thou, art LORD alone; thou hast made heaven, the heaven of heavens, with all their host, Earth, and all things that are therein, the seas, and all that is therein, and thou *preservest them all*; and the host of heaven worshippeth thee. (Nehemiah 9:6)

Within the first fraction of a second from the creation event, the laws of physics governing the universe existed; specifically, a flat space-time, general relativity, special relativity, the first law of thermodynamics, quantum mechanics, the four fundamental forces, energy/mass equivalence or $E=mc^2$, and a language to describe it all, mathematics. This evident order of the universe at 10^{-32} of a second from the start of time is fixed; it leaves no room for random evolution over time.

These early creation phenomena suggest Nehemiah 9:6a is correct in the claim that the God of the Bible made the heaven and heaven of heavens and their entire host. In this verse, the Creator has now added the claim of preserver or sustainer of the structure for and of life for all that was created to his many accomplishments.

This is a major attribute of the Creator for the theist. A theist is one who believes in a God who not only created but also governs *and* directs the universe. A deist is one who believes in a God who created the universe and allows it to govern itself through natural processes to do what we see in the universe today. The Creator's claim of being the sustainer of the universe suggests that he influences the operations and conditions of Earth, as the theist understands him to be. As the sustainer, God controls the entire ecosystem, from establishing the landscape and topography above and below the oceans to the positioning of the continents through plate tectonics, controlling both the climate and weather through the atmosphere, jet streams, oceans, heat of the sun and cold of the poles to sustain life on Earth.

Let's go back to the overall heavens or cosmos for a moment, particularly to what scientists refer to as the flatness/oldness problem. It is considered a problem in part because an explanation for how the initial flatness occurred has not yet been found. Another part of the problem is the fact that the universe has remained finely tuned to be flat for 13.8 billion years despite the lack of any "natural" explanation. In addition, the finely tuned cosmological constant of the increasingly accelerating universe has not affected the flatness. That is fine-tuning on top of fine-tuning.

I am not invoking the "God of the gaps" logic to explain how this takes place, simply reminding the reader it is the God of the Bible that pointed out the existence of both phenomena. A complete future understanding of these phenomena will not change the fact that they were declared in the Bible many centuries ago.

The use of the present tense in many of the expanding universe claims indicates the Creator's role is a continuous one. In review, a flat universe is based upon the uniform distribution of energy/mass that continues to match critical density at creation. This flatness was proclaimed by the Bible through the metaphor of a tent lying on the ground in the process of erecting the tent. Considering the

Increased genera follow all ten mass extinctions

great expansion of the universe from the size of an atom to the immeasurable universe of today, how is it possible for the universe to remain flat? The current flatness of the universe required maintenance as stars and galaxies formed while space expanded and accelerated at various speeds and vast distances. Yet, its relative density has remained flat from the moment of creation.

> The black curve shows a critical density case that matches the WMAP-based concordance model, which has density = 447,225,917,218,507,401,284,016 gm/cc at 1 nanosecond after the Big Bang. Adding only 0.2 gm/cc to this 447-sextillion gm/cc causes the Big Crunch to be right now! Taking away 0.2 gm/cc gives a model with a matter density Ω_M that is too low for our observations. Thus, the density 1 nanosecond after the Big Bang was set to an accuracy of better than 1 part in 2235 sextillion. Even earlier it was set to an accuracy better than 1 part in 10^{59}! Since if the density is slightly high, the Universe will die in an early Big Crunch, this is called the "oldness" problem in cosmology. And since the critical density Universe has flat spatial geometry, it is also called the "flatness" problem—or the "flatness-oldness" problem.[33]

Thus, a small deviation from the perfectly flat value would produce havoc for the formation of the universe. This is a balancing act of galactic proportions! A difference of only two-tenths of a gram per cubic centimeter across the universe determines if the universe is flat, open, or closed. The question is how did the universe get this

---

33   Edward Wright, "Flatness-Oldness Problem," *Astro.ucla.edu*, http://www.astro.ucla.edu/~wright/cosmo_03.htm#FO.

old without destroying itself by a slight change in its density over the past 13.8 billion years? This conundrum is called the oldness/flatness problem by cosmologists. God claimed unequivocally to have laid out space-time flat. It also has to be sustained. Regardless of the means by which it was done, science has verified his claim of flatness then and now. And he has maintained that flatness with incredible precision.

Below is the current measurement of the density of the universe after one nanosecond after the Big Bang, shown in a slightly different manner. The difference of matter per cubic centimeter is flat based upon the readings below.

Open—447,225,917,218,507,401,284,015.8 grams/cc
Flat—447,225,917,218,507,401,284,016.0 grams/cc
Closed—447,225,917,218,507,401,284,016.2 grams/cc [34]

While expanding the universe, and maintaining critical density, some planning was in order so that the intelligent inhabitants of the new Earth would have a sufficient amount of stored energy to maintain a very advanced lifestyle. The largest source of energy in use that I am referring to are fossil fuels; namely, natural gas, coal, and crude oil. The other source is nuclear energy that was stored in the joining of atoms through stellar nuclear fusion in stars. This energy is released through the subsequent splitting of atoms. This is no accident; both were planned. Without these stored energy sources there would have been no Industrial Revolution. We would be limited to burning plant products for a short period of time before we destroyed the plants and ourselves.

Fossil fuels are derived from geologic deposits of decayed plant and animals formed through pressure and heat. Before the plant

---

[34] Edward Wright, "Flatness-Oldness Problem," *Astro.ucla.edu*, http://www.astro.ucla.edu/~wright/cosmo_03.htm#FO.

and animals can decay into the air, they are covered by layers of sediment. The future oil and natural gas in the sediment is then sealed by impervious rock, under high pressure for millions of years. So, in order for the civilized society to have the necessary energy deposits needed today, planning occurred hundreds of millions of years ago.

According to the Genesis account of day three, some seven hundred million years ago, during the Proterozoic Eon, plant life was established by the Creator. And by day six during the Cenozoic Period, the Creator acknowledged the entire face (surface) of the Earth was covered with vegetation. Between the biblical day three and the acknowledgement about vegetation in the biblical day six, the Carboniferous Period occurred some three hundred fifty million years ago and about three hundred fifty million years after the biblical account of the establishment of plant life. The Carboniferous is a period of exceptional plant production on Earth. During this period of about sixty million years, the bulk of the raw material for fossil fuels on the planet was produced.

These fossil fuels are found on every continent on Earth, proof of the Creator's claim of an Earth covered by plant life. The Bible predicts God is the purveyor of the layers of the atmosphere, thus making him controller of the Earth's prehistoric climate, which facilitated the explosion of plant life. He was also the architect of the Permian mass extinction that followed. The Permian is the greatest mass extinction of record, when 95 percent of marine life and 70 percent of land animals, along with plants, died in a relatively short time.

These fossil beds are part of the vast energy reserves we extract from the Earth today. The largest oil reservoir in the southwestern United States, covering part of west Texas and New Mexico, is called the Permian Basin. It contains the thickest deposit of Permian aged rock on Earth. The Carboniferous Period for plants and the Cambrian Period for marine life provided the means for this vast reserve of energy. The Cambrian is the period of abundant life the Creator established in the Genesis account of day five.

Plate tectonics play an important role in the formation of oil and gas deposits. Of course, we understand that the Creator is behind the movement of plate tectonics through established natural processes, as referred to in day three of the Days of Creation chapter. The sustainer God made these deposits of energy for the benefit of future humankind.

Having an abundant reserve of combustible fuel for life adds to the extensive list of unique attributes of planet Earth. A habitable planet requires an enormous stored energy source. An estimated ninety-six million barrels, or 4,032,000,000 gallons, *per day* is extracted from the Earth for humans to use. Humans have been extracting daily quantities like this for decades! "Give us this day, our daily bread." This daily provision of fuel is exclusively for humans; the animals do not have the intellect to use fossil fuels. This contradicts the naturalists' worldview that humans are not special. Only God can provide this daily provision by such grand design and scale.

The Creator provided the essentials for mankind to live and flourish. He also is the source for minerals to endow mankind with riches. All gold, silver, and diamonds are brought up from beneath the Earth by volcanic and tectonic plate activity.

With a finite amount of energy, the universe was created to live and die, having a beginning and an end. On a continuing basis, our sun is dying that we can continually live. Plants and animals have died that we can have fossil fuels to keep warm in the winter and even cool in summer. The stars lived and died to provide the elements for the "clay" from which man is made by God.

The concept of death provided the means by which Adam was created. Adam's sin is not the original sin or death. Lucifer and one third of the angels had sinned and was separated from God before Adam was created. The idea of dying for the benefit and even the life of another is as old as the universe in the mind of the Creator. What we observe in the universe is in concert with the scripture,

Increased genera follow all ten mass extinctions

and God's plan for the death of Christ was established before the foundation of the *kosmos*. *Kosmos* is the original Greek word translated to "world." Why is the world so surprised that Jesus died for humanity?

> And all that dwell upon the Earth shall worship him, whose names are not written in the book of life of the Lamb *slain from the foundation of the world*. (Revelation 13:8)

Entropy

> Lift up your eyes to the heavens, and look upon Earth beneath: for the heavens shall vanish away like smoke, and Earth shall wax old like a garment. (Isaiah 51:6a)

According to the scriptures and observation of creation, entropy was established from creation. Entropy is represented by the metaphor of vanishing smoke, increasing disorder until it disappears. Here in the Book of Isaiah, we are instructed to lift up our eyes to the heavens to understand a different message. The heavens refer to everywhere. Upon observation beyond physics, there are many forms of entropy other than the second law of thermodynamics. Humans of Isaiah's time could not examine both the heavens and Earth *fully* to understand and verify God's claims.

Today, the claim is validated using the technology that allows us to scrutinize both the heavens and Earth. As usual, God is not asking for some "blind" faith. The command is to search and find evidence that affirms he is wrong or to glorify God as Creator and learn that this magnificent universe is coming to an end. He predicted there would be signs. Looking to the heavens shows the evidence of an expanding universe, manifesting how the laws of thermodynamics are taking their toll on the universe. It also shows it is indeed expanding and even accelerating, growing thinner like rising, vanishing smoke.

Creation with a finite amount of energy in an expanding universe and preserving the first law of thermodynamics ensures that the universe will die. The inevitable natural death for the universe was not determined at the time of Adam, but at the creation event itself. Before the discovery of the CMB radiation, scientists were able to calculate its temperature with great accuracy. This is an astounding accomplishment to say the least, to measure the thermal loss of an expanding universe. The then theorized afterglow in the microwave spectrum of the CMB was estimated in 1948 to be about 5 Kelvin.

The accurate estimate of the CMB temperature verifies the second law of thermodynamics has been intact from the creation event to now. The second law of thermodynamics is the law of entropy. When this afterglow, known as the cosmic microwave background radiation, was discovered in the mid-1960s it measured 2.7 Kelvin. This is rock solid proof entropy started at creation, not at the fall of Adam. The initial temperature of the creation event (the Big Bang) has been diminishing with the constant expansion of the universe approaching a state of thermal equilibrium. The transfer of energy is continuing throughout the universe. When everything reaches the same temperature, the universe, in essence, will die.

The same scripture instructs us to examine Earth for evidence that it has been worn as a garment. At the time this scripture was written, Earth's resources were abundant, and the habitats of many animals were plentiful and healthy. Today, our natural resources are being diminished and replaced with pollution and waste material. Earth is showing it is being worn out by our use of it, like an old worn garment. And if Earth does not survive over time, neither will its inhabitants.

Contrary to the limited existence of the natural universe, the spiritual salvation God has established for humans is eternal. Unlike all other creation, humans were created with a natural body and a spiritual existence, in God's image. Humans are special and have a hope that no other creature possesses.

> And all the host of heaven shall be dissolved, and the heavens shall be rolled together as a scroll: and all their host shall fall down, as the leaf falleth off from the vine, and as a falling fig from the fig tree. (Isaiah 34:4)

When the natural universe, along with its laws, energy, and subsequent events cease to exist, time (this age) as we know it will also cease. The Creator declares he will fold up this operation, and they all shall be changed. The falling of the leaf and fig represent the continual death of the host of heaven, particularly the stars. The Bible uses two separate metaphors to describe how the host will fall down. Just as the leaves of a tree fall one at a time, and the figs of a fig tree fall one at a time, likewise the stars will fall down, will stop shining. The most spectacular example that is witnessed today of the stellar deaths are supernova explosions. The image below of the Crab Nebula, which was once a star, was taken by the Hubble telescope. Its stunning beauty is the result of its death. White dwarf stars are another example of the death of stars.

Crab Nebula - Hubble Image

The end of the universe is not doom and gloom. If he created the first universe, he can change it to be what he wants it to be. According to the Bible, the end of the universe as we know it is not an absolute end. In Luke 18:30, Mark 10:30, and other scriptures, the Bible also claims there is a world to come that is different from the one we experience now. It appears that this world is only part of the plan of the Creator.

> Who shall not receive manifold more in this present time, and in the world to come life everlasting. (Luke 18:30)

Thermodynamic Entropy

Thermodynamics powers the operation of the entire universe through the heat (energy) transfer that drives everything. The two fundamental laws of thermodynamics are universal in their operation throughout time. The first law of thermodynamics states energy can be neither created nor destroyed, and the amount of energy in the universe is constant. The original amount of energy at creation is all the energy there is in the universe. It does not evolve into more energy, but it is being transferred constantly. Energy is released or absorbed when the bonds between atoms are created or destroyed. Nuclear reactors are powered by the splitting of atoms, while the stars are powered by the combination of atoms. They transfer all of their energy through light and heat until they run out of fuel. This is why stars die but energy is not destroyed.

> And, Thou, Lord, in the beginning hast laid the foundation of the Earth; and the heavens are the works of thine hands: They shall perish; but thou remainest; and *they all shall wax old as doth a garment.* (Hebrews 1:10-11)

The second law of thermodynamics states that the entropy of the universe can only increase. The universe has to be finite because it had a beginning, even though it is immeasurable, as the Bible declared thousands of years ago. This entropy has been taking place from the beginning of time and creation when the universe was in its lowest state of entropy. Due to the finite amount of energy along with the first and second law of thermodynamics, the universe is mandated by the laws of physics—which have been in place since the first moment of creation—to eventually die.

Entropy has been scientifically affirmed to verify the passage of time. The arrow of time demonstrates it is the greatest of all the laws of physics by not allowing any other law to reverse itself. A broken egg cannot be unbroken despite the best efforts of all the king's horses and all the king's men. Once an event passes from the present into the past, it cannot be reversed.

The complexity we witness in the universe came about contrary to the second law of thermodynamics by the hands of a causal agent called the Creator, just as all advancements in which humankind is the causal agent can be traced to humankind. In fact, the patent system was constructed to protect inventors of complexity. There is no pure, natural way to the complexity of the universe, as promoted by naturalists. A naturalist is one who holds a worldview that only natural elements and physical laws and rules govern the structure and operation of the universe. In their explanation of this so-called natural method to complexity, they insert pseudo-causal agents such as the so-called "Goldilocks conditions" and "nature" to account for the complexity of the universe.

Let's say you come to play a game of golf. You pull out your driver and walk up to the tee box, only to find a ball sitting on a tee in your preferred spot and elevation. You ask your partner if he placed the ball there, and he says that it's nice to play on a course that has Goldilocks conditions; where everything is always just right. You will not be inclined to accept that explanation of how the ball got there. A golf ball on a tee is not a complex phenomenon. As an intelligent being, you would think that a human did the simple task of placing the tee and the ball on it.

A causal phenomenon like the initial conditions of extreme low entropy at the beginning of the universe should not be explained by a reference to Goldilocks conditions. There are a tremendous number of possibilities for the golf ball other than on a tee in the tee box, which is the essence of entropy. The God of the Bible has predicted we would find the then-unknown phenomenon called entropy in the life and death of the stars and planets, as well as humans, who all grow, age, and die.

Educational (Information) Entropy

Generally speaking, entropy is referred to as movement toward disorder and uncertainty, but it is not limited to physics. When we look at the intelligent life of humankind, we find other "general entropies" that follow the same principle of disorder when left to its own unnatural existence.

> Study to shew thyself approved unto God, a workman that needeth not to be ashamed, rightly dividing the word of truth. (2 Timothy 2:15)

The Bible commands us to study and learn the Bible. The high-tech life and knowledge of humankind cannot go on without continual maintenance and growth. From the early days of humankind, knowledge has been learned and passed on to other humans, which has benefited society. This general knowledge has accumulated and has been shared verbally with more and more humans to the point of mental limitations of individuals in a way that stymies the advancement of humankind. The limits of the capacity and ability to retain information in our mind necessitated books. Books allow humans to retain, access, and transfer more knowledge than by the limits of the mind alone.

The limited capacity of collective memory brought about the need for written language so that the knowledge above the mental capacity of individuals and/or collective humankind could grow, be stored, and then shared on a larger scale. Now the language has to be taught so that the information contained in the written record can be communicated and shared. This is the beginning of an advanced education.

Education today is fundamental to the society in which we live. In education, entropy of a different sort also manifests, because if energy, in the form of preserving existing knowledge, educating new humans, building upon existing knowledge, and preserving that new knowledge in new books and storage methods, is not maintained constantly, our educational system will deteriorate, along with the complexity of our society. If we stop putting effort (energy) into the operation called education, disorder will deteriorate our total knowledge, and society will revert back to the limited mental capacity of an earlier age. Education is a fundamental element of all that we do as a society. Many in the world today make the task of education a career in and of itself. We have the structures of lower education, generally termed grade school, and higher education, generally termed as colleges or universities. Educators in these and other institutions are employed to inhibit the unnatural entropy of knowledge.

Economic Entropy

Entropy is not a completely negative concept despite its propensity for disorder. As the Creator of the laws of physics, God uses these fundamental laws to sustain his creation. He established entropy to provide for his highest creation, humankind. Without entropy, no society could survive. On the surface, entropy seems like a never-ending process of having to redo everything.

> Vanity of vanities, saith the Preacher, vanity of vanities; all is vanity. What profit hath a man of all his labour which he taketh under the sun? (Ecclesiastes 1:2–3)

Like Solomon, the wise of this world wrestle with why and how the Creator established his world, and why and how he included entropy as a part of it. Contrary to its tendency toward disorder, the Creator established entropy for the economic benefit of society first and then for the individual who is a part of society. What a strange method to sustain life for humans. It is difficult to find any occupation that is not established to overcome some form of entropy, either directly or indirectly.

Increased genera follow all ten mass extinctions

The economies of the world are built upon and sustained by entropy. Without entropy, automobiles would last forever, and we would still be driving the original automobiles built over a hundred years ago. Why would we need to build new ones if the first ones never wore out? Because everything deteriorates, people have jobs to make new products to replace the worn-out products. In addition, society needs the service industry to service and repair the equipment to keep entropy at bay as long as possible. Everybody needs a place to live, which requires someone to build it and keep it from deteriorating. Even our health requires maintenance because it also deteriorates with time. Entropy *forces* us all to serve one another to maintain life. We crowd the highways and roads every workday on our way to serve someone else, either directly or indirectly. We are in constant need to *replace* fuel, food, clothing and other essentials used to maintain life.

The many areas in which entropy is evident demonstrate the necessity of a management operation to keep it operating smoothly. Is there any reason to think that Earth's varied, interdependent ecosystems can be set up and operate on their own without a manager? From the beginning of creation, entropy has been a part of the operation of the universe. Economic, moral, and educational entropy are not part of the natural law of the physical world. However, all forms of entropy we observe has been described by the Bible.

Entropy for Life

Entropy existed in the Garden of Eden from day one. Entropy is required to get energy from food via the digestion process for all animals. Entropy is required to do any kind of work, from the initial creation all the way through the process where the plants receive photons to carry out photosynthesis. Before the fall, Adam had to eat to keep from dying.

> And God blessed them, and God said unto them, Be fruitful, and multiply, and replenish the Earth, and subdue it: (Genesis 1:28a)

The fact that the garden needed tending demonstrates energy had to be exerted to prevent disorder from taking over. Work was required by the Creator before the fall of Adam. The command to subdue Earth in the first chapter of Genesis verse twenty-seven uses the Hebrew word *kabash,* which means "to force, bring into, to keep under." This shows from the outset there was opposition to the goals of humankind, indicating entropy is everywhere, which required work to keep the order of the garden. The very act of eating requires entropy to digest plants or meat. From this and the previous example, it is evident that entropy extends beyond the second law of thermodynamics. Solomon the King of Israel and writer of the Book of Ecclesiastes could not see why God had set up the world he observed around him. Solomon's perception of entropy was of vain repetition as shown in his biblical statement "vanity of vanities; all is vanity." Almost all of Solomon's problems with God in the book of Ecclesiastes pertain to entropy of some type. He accomplished something significant, and it deteriorated with age and was taken from him at the end of his life to become the possession of another. The tendency for the progression of disorder caused Solomon to view all his work as vanity or meaningless.

> I have seen all the works that are done under the sun; and, behold, all is vanity and vexation of spirit. (Ecclesiastes 1:14)

Entropy was part of God's original condition for humankind before the original fall and the start of moral entropy in humankind.

Increased genera follow all ten mass extinctions

The fall of man was not a surprise to the Creator. God did not create Adam to live forever. This is evident from the fact that Adam needed to eat from the tree of life to live forever as a natural human before the fall. If Adam were created to live forever, for what purpose would the Creator have put the tree of life in the garden before the fall? Adam had a choice to eat of the tree of life and live forever. God took Adam and Eve out of the garden before they could eat of the tree of life and live naturally, forever, in a fallen state.

After the fall, the tree of life still had the original power to give life without end, which is why Adam and Eve were forcefully prevented from having access to it. For the tree of life to be an option before the fall, death was inevitable. God promised Adam that if he ate of the tree of good and evil, he would surely die. That day, Adam was separated from God (spiritual death), separated from his spiritual life source.

Chapter 6

Ecology of Earth

Some think God created all the laws and parameters of the physical universe and then set them on autopilot mode, after which everything formed and sustained itself. Observable evidence of the Earth's uniqueness and its operation does not lend itself to such thinking. In the following, I will examine claims made by the God of the Bible and compare them to the heavens and Earth that requires a sustainer.

Make It Rain

> Wherefore, when I came, was there no man? when I called, was there none to answer? Is my hand shortened at all, that it cannot redeem? or have I no power to deliver? behold, *at my rebuke I dry up the sea, I make the rivers a wilderness:* their fish stinketh, because there is no water, and dieth for thirst. (Isaiah 50:2)

The best example of Isaiah 50:2 is the African Sahara. The largest nonpolar desert on Earth was once an extremely large lake with rivers until it dried up. The great Death Valley desert in the United States was a lake at one time as well. So was the great Atacama Desert in Chile, considered the driest place on Earth. The Sahara once had the largest lakes on Earth, the largest called Mega Chad. It was also home to many rivers discovered with ground-penetrating radar from space by the Space Shuttle Radar Topography Mission.

The Bible's descriptions of the phenomenon of drying up the sea and rivers have been affirmed by scientific observation. The layers of the atmosphere, plate tectonics, Earth's orbit, and their subsequent control by the Creator (all of which are alluded to in the Bible) all form part of the methods used to accomplish this feat.

On the surface, it might seem that turning a body of water into a desert and killing all the fish in the process is a waste. Without a big picture perspective of the operation of Earth, the deserts seem to be a wasteland, but the Creator knows otherwise. Just as the death of stars brings life, the death of these bodies of water still produce life today.

The Sahara was once the world's largest freshwater lake along with surrounding lakes and rivers. The Creator dried this wetland, as proclaimed in the above scripture, to help Earth sustain life. Satellite observations have revealed that an astronomical amount of the remains of water life accumulated over millions of years by plankton, called diatomite, permeate the dust of the Sahara. Diatoms are a common type of marine plankton. Their skeletons are composed of silica (silicon dioxide), a very durable substance. Since diatom skeletons are highly porous, diatomite is lightweight and ideal for being carried by the wind.

The remains of the plankton are picked up by the frequent wind storms and carried across the Atlantic Ocean to other continents, specifically the Amazon region of South America. The diatomite is a rich source of phosphorous, the second most abundant mineral

Increased genera follow all ten mass extinctions

in the body and present in every cell. It also makes a great fertilizer. The phosphate mixes with the rain in the rainforest of the Amazon to produce the largest concentration of vegetation on Earth. With lightning producing nitrogen in the clouds, the greatest gardener on Earth has a garden he sustains. The Amazon basin is critical to Earth's climate, and it serves this purpose thanks to the foresight of the Creator, who, through a complex chain of events, created life in the Amazon from the seeming desolation of the Sahara. Directly and indirectly, the Amazon basin contributes a tremendous amount of oxygen for all air-breathing creatures on Earth. Who would have thought the great dust storms of the Sahara help us all to breathe better?

The symmetry that is evident in the early universe is also found in the operation of Earth. That symmetry is evident in the balance of Earth's dry, lifeless deserts interacting with green and lush life-producing regions. The dust and minerals of the Mojave Desert and mountains assist the food production of the Great Plains of the United States. Though they may not seem so, deserts are indeed key players in producing rain and food across the globe. As the Creator and Sustainer of life on Earth, God needed deserts on Earth at all times for life to flourish.

Why does Earth need more deserts? Dust is needed for Earth's rain process! Shocked? Consider this: dust in rain falling in the state of California has been traced to the deserts of Asia and Africa, carried by the jet stream and upper atmospheric winds. The dust from the Sahara assists the rainfall in many regions on Earth besides the Amazon. All that was needed for Earth to thrive was wisely determined long before humankind came to learn of its value. This is another example of the Creator/Sustainer at work.

> Who can number the clouds in wisdom? or who can stay the bottles of heaven, when the *dust* groweth into *hardness*, and the *clods* cleave fast together? (Job 38:37–38)

God is asking Job who can keep the bottles of water (a metaphor for clouds that hold water) in heaven from falling when the water grows too heavy attached to a particle (often dust that floats with the clouds). A rain cloud that produces one inch of rain over a single square mile of land (640 acres) carries and delivers via air mail 17,378,560 gallons of water, weighing a total of 144,937,190 pounds! That's 2,898 eighteen-wheeler loads of fifty thousand pounds of water each! That is only one inch of water for one square mile. Who can hold and carry that amount of water and float it through the air? Think of one inch of water for an entire city or state! The Creator can deliver *more* than that amount through the atmosphere: drop it to the ground without knocking the petals from the flowers that need it.

> Raindrops begin forming when water vapor condenses on micrometer-sized particles of dust floating in the atmosphere. The dust particles grow to millimeter-sized droplets, which are heavy enough to begin falling. As they fall, the droplets accumulate more and more moisture, until they become the large raindrops that we see here on the ground.[35]

The Creator is describing a long-hidden feature in the formation of rain. Raindrops form when water vapor condenses on fine particles of dust suspended in the atmosphere. The drops clod together and become heavier. Before falling to the ground, these drops of water can also freeze, as the passage above describes, growing in hardness. Both the words "growth" and "hardness" used in the passage mean to cast or to give shape. Water in a liquid

---

35 "How Raindrops Form," *American Physical Society*, http://physics.aps.org/story/v7/st14.

Increased genera follow all ten mass extinctions

state is dynamic and shapeless. Only by freezing can it take a fixed shape. At higher elevations, the temperature of thunderstorms in the troposphere, the lowest atmospheric layer, can range from -49 to -103 degrees Fahrenheit. As the temperature falls, the frozen rain thaws in warmer, lower levels and ultimately falls to the ground as water. These are the droplets that the scripture said would harden. If the thunderstorm is high enough, the drops can freeze and fall to Earth as hail. Using mass spectrometers, scientists have been able to pinpoint this phenomenon. Only the Creator could know such high-level activity in the clouds to confront Job about it in 1800 BC.

Dust is vitally important to Earth, and not only because of rain. It also reflects sunlight away from Earth and is a major contributor to the sky's blue color. The various colors of the sunset are influenced by the dust in the upper atmosphere. The mysteries of creation seem to go on and on, and their revelations are recorded in the ancient word of the Bible. It is simply amazing.

It is he that buildeth his *stories* in the heaven, and hath founded his troop in Earth; he that calleth for the waters of the sea, and poureth them out upon the face of Earth: The Lord is his name. (Amos 9:6)

God declares there are stories or steps in the heaven, one upon the other. This refers to the atmospheric layers of the first heaven. This first heaven is not mentioned directly in the Bible as such. The Greek word *ouranos* is translated as "air" and "heaven," as in James 5:18, which states that heaven gave rain, and Earth produced fruit. The highest heaven found in Deuteronomy 10:14 as the residence of God suggests there is a lower one. This highest or third heaven is referenced by the Apostle Paul in 2 Corinthians 12:2, where most scholars believe Paul was describing himself as caught up to the third heaven. The second heaven is considered the one between the first and third heavens, being the celestial heaven of the planets and stars.

God determined this reference by founding or establishing a troop on Earth. This word "troop" is the Hebrew word *aguddah*, meaning "vault" (of the heavens) and "firmament" (binding Earth to the heavens). Binding to the Earth indicates being bound by gravity. The stories are part of the one heaven, its layers of the atmosphere. These layers are the troposphere, stratosphere, mesosphere, thermosphere, exosphere, and on into outer space. Just as the Bible predicted, science has confirmed the atmosphere has layers or stories. No one can determine there are atmospheric layers merely by looking into the sky. This is yet another divine revelation of a vital natural phenomenon needed to sustain life.

The atmosphere is the primary vehicle for the total interconnected systems that promote Earth's dynamic, life-giving features. Rain is only one of the systems. The energy from the sun is distributed across Earth's surface to regulate its temperature by cooling the equator via evaporation and transferring that heat to the poles from the equator.

> For by him were all things created, that are in heaven, and that are in Earth, visible and invisible, whether they be thrones, or dominions, or principalities, or powers: all things were created by him, and for him. (Colossians 1:16)

Earth's storied or layered atmosphere is another example of the invisible creation referred to in the Book of Colossians. God uses the layers of the atmosphere to protect Earth from overheating during the day and freezing at night. They also protect the planet from meteors by burning them up before they reach the surface and protect all life from the sun's UV rays.

> When he uttereth his voice, there is a multitude of waters in the heavens, and he causeth the vapours to ascend from the ends of Earth. (Jeremiah 10:13a)

> Hast thou not known? hast thou not heard, that the everlasting God, the LORD, the *Creator of the ends of Earth*, fainteth not, neither is weary? there is no searching of his understanding. (Isaiah 40:28)

The utterance of his voice is a reference to his control. Liquid, solid, and vapor forms of water exist in the clouds—the multitude of water in the heavens. It is hard to comprehend that one inch of rain covering one square mile, which is 17,378,560 gallons of water weighing a total of 144,937,190 pounds, can come from a floating cloud. Once again, only through recent scientific discoveries have we been able to verify this assertion.

Some have interpreted the reference to the "ends" of Earth in these scriptures as meaning that the Bible is saying Earth is flat. Psalm 19:6 is a reference to the sun's orbital circuit with ends. Does this say that the Milky Way is flat? No. The orbital reference is to a circle with ends, which is an elliptical circle. Earth is an elliptical circle, so it has ends. Pictures of the wonderful blue planet from space make it appear to be a perfect sphere, but it is not. Its shape is classified as oblate, spheroid, or ellipsoid; it is not a true circle. Earth bulges at the equator due in part to its one-thousand-mile-per-hour rotation. It is called the equatorial bulge. When measured across the equatorial plane, Earth's diameter is 26.5 miles more than when measured using the north/south pole diameter. The rotation and ocean waters create this bulge at the equator, which are the ends of its elliptical shape.

Just as the Bible predicted a planet with ends, it also predicted this area near the equator is where most of the world's rain originates in the form of invisible water vapor. This is a major part of Earth's thermal machine that controls the temperature and climate through the transfer of heat for the whole Earth. God described this phenomenon in about 700 BC. As the Creator said in the Bible, the water vapor ascends from the region closest to the sun and the hottest area of the planet, which produces an enormous amount of evaporation to be carried to various areas of the planet via the layer of the atmosphere, to be returned to the oceans from which they came via rain and rivers. This tremendous amount of water vapor is invisible to the naked eye and can only be seen with infrared satellite instruments. The prophet Jeremiah could not simply have sat on the shore and witnessed this phenomenon. Only by divine revelation was this made known.

> All the rivers run into the sea; yet the sea is not full; unto the place from whence the rivers come, thither they return again. (Ecclesiastes 1:7)

According to scientists, the oceans contribute about 80 percent of all global precipitation. This is an enormous amount of water that is "air mailed" to thirsty plants and animals, which are themselves made of a high percentage of water. This great thirst must be satisfied with fresh water, which comprises only 1 percent of Earth's water supply. The main source of this global fresh water supply is salt water. Salt water is unfit—even deadly—for land-based plants and animals. The process of evaporation separates the bulk of the salt but utilizes small particles of salt along with dust to produce rain. The latent heat of evaporation also helps to keep the planet's overall temperature cool by transferring the heat of the sun from the equator into the atmosphere and to colder atmospheric regions.

Thunder and Lightning

The cause of thunder was a mystery for many millennia. Early theories included various divine causes and cloud collisions, and even a theory that lightning produced a vacuum reigned among supposedly learned men. It turns out the real explanation was exactly what the Creator declared in scripture.

> It was not until the turn of the 20th century that consensus was reached in the scientific community about the origin of thunder. Thunder is the sound generated by lightning produced by a sudden and violent expansion of super-heated air in and along the electrical discharge channel path. Thunder can be a sharp or rumbling sound. A sudden increase in pressure and temperature causes surrounding air to expand violently at a rate faster than the speed of sound, similar to a sonic boom. The shock wave extends outward for the first 30 feet (10 m), after which it becomes an ordinary sound wave called thunder.[36]

God challenged Job concerning his knowledge of creation by asking him if he understood thunder. About four thousand years later, we discovered the answer is actually in the very question God asked Job. There is no "crash" or "clap" of thunder. It is not the

---

36 Jim Allsop, "The Science of Thunder," *National Lightning Safety Institute*, http://www.lightningsafety.com/nlsi_info/thunder2.html.

collision of air, as theorized by many, but the separating of the air at such a speed that it creates a sonic boom while separating. The sudden presence of an electrical charge at a temperature over 25,000 degrees Celsius superheats the moisture/air combination to spread at a supersonic rate, producing a sonic boom.

> Also can any understand the *spreadings of the clouds*, ~~or~~ the noise of his tabernacle? (Job 36:29)

In the translation from the original Hebrew to English, the word "or" was added by translators in an attempt to clarify the statement. The preposition "or" could imply that these are two separate statements when actually the first refers to the second. It originally read, "Can any understand the spreading of the clouds, the noise of his tabernacle?" Based upon today's scientific knowledge, the better word to add would be "is." It is the spreading of the air (clouds) by lightning that causes thunder, just as the scripture predicted.

There are several types of lightning, including ground to cloud, blue jet, dark lightning, ball, and sprites, some of which can be seen by anyone on the ground. We are all familiar with ground to cloud lightning, the most common type. We can look into the distant sky and witness lightning as it races across and within the clouds. On rare occasions, ball lightning is seen. However, there is a type of a lightning the Bible declares was not seen at the time of the writing of Job.

> And *now* men see not the bright light which is in the clouds: but the wind passeth, and cleanseth them. (Job 37:21)

Increased genera follow all ten mass extinctions

The bright light spoken of in Job 37:21 is not the Aurora Borealis or Aurora Australis, also known as the northern and southern polar lights. These polar lights can be readily seen by the naked eye if there is no cloud cover. Rather, there is a class of lightning only seen above the clouds in the upper atmosphere where jet planes fly, called elves, sprites, blue jets, and gigantic jets. Elves and sprites are reddish, and blue jets are blue in color. The scripture correctly declares for a time these bright lights high above the clouds would not be seen; however, high elevation flight and high-tech devices have given us the ability to witness these phenomena.

Jet pilots began to witness the lightning that rose from the top of the clouds toward the upper atmosphere and lasted only milliseconds. When they first reported it, the jet pilots' account was not believed, but because of the number of accounts, serious scientific inquiry was initiated. With extremely high-speed cameras from the vantage point of space (thanks to the lost crew of the Columbia Space Shuttle, and later on the International Space Station), images of sprites were captured. These sprites accompany the extreme lightning in the high clouds of severe tropical storms and subsequently extend high above the clouds to the ionosphere, the last atmospheric layer before outer space.

These upper atmosphere types of lightning are also known as transient luminous events, which are a part of regulating the global electric circuit between the Earth and the ionosphere. Lightning strikes the Earth an estimated one hundred times every second to help regulate this flow of electricity.

> Lightning is not an event isolated within the confines of a thunderstorm. It is part of a massive electrical circuit that literally covers the globe. The voltage difference between ground and ionosphere is 200,000 to 500,000 volts (200 to 500 kV). Even in fair weather, a slight current of 2 pA

(picoamps, or 0.0000000000001 A) flows from every square meter of ground upward to the ionosphere. Thunderstorms alone send 1 A of current skyward. Indeed, the flash rate for a storm is directly related to its current flow.[37]

Life depends upon an electric Earth. The molten foundation, discussed in the earlier reference to the creation (making) of the Earth and tectonic plates, is part of the source of the magnetic field that surrounds the Earth. Scientists theorize the spinning of Earth's solid core within the molten mantle creates the constant external magnetic field that protects life on Earth from the sun's harmful charged solar wind. This magnetic field constantly generates electricity that will flow from the Earth to space.

There are two fundamental fields that make up the universe; the first one was discussed earlier in this book as a matter field, which is the Higgs field. The other field is a force field whose effect can be seen with the naked eye. The manifestation of the force field is the northern and southern polar lights, also known as the Aurora Borealis or Aurora Australis.

There are an estimated three million lightning strikes per day on Earth. This lightning is also necessary for all plants because it produces nitrate, which dissolves into the rain and falls to Earth to fertilize the plant world. Nitrates help plants to produce seeds for the continuation of life, as proclaimed by the Creator to reproduce after their kind. The plants absorb the nitrates through their root system and reproduce. We, in turn, eat the plants and seeds to receive the life-giving nutrients required to build proteins and DNA. The Sustainer is working in the stories of the atmosphere he created to sustain Earth's creatures.

---

37 http://science.nasa.gov/science-news/science-at-nasa/lis/lis_4

Increased genera follow all ten mass extinctions

When he uttereth his voice, there is a multitude of waters in the heavens, and causeth the vapours to ascend from the ends of Earth; he maketh lightnings with rain, and bringeth forth the wind out of his treasures. (Jeremiah 10:13)

Now that we recognize that only God knew the actual process of rain and the actual cause of thunder, we can be assured that he creates the lightning that causes the thunder and accommodates the rain. We have the dust, oceanic evaporation, the cold upper atmosphere for condensation, and collisions of charged particles producing static electricity or lightning. Now, Earth needs a medium to transport the entire operation from one geographical location and elevation to another at a specified season, due to Earth's precise tilt caused by the strategically placed moon. God brought out his wind from his treasures or storehouses, which are for the benefits of his creation. Around 1000 BC, God affirmed there was a circular wind that did some strange things. No one could verify what God was talking about until the 1920s. Today, these global circular winds are called the jet streams.

The wind goeth toward the south, and turneth about unto the north; it whirleth about continually, and the wind returneth again according to his circuits. (Ecclesiastes 1:6)

The control of the weather and life-giving precipitation on Earth is driven mainly by the jet streams that circle the Earth. These jet streams are what the Bible is referring to in Ecclesiastes 1:6. They turn to flow south immediately and then turn to flow north before making a circuit around Earth at thirty-two thousand to fifty-two thousand feet above sea level. This phenomenon is not visible by looking to the sky or climbing the highest mountain.

All jet streams have a meandering shape to their continual circuits. The Bible talks of the jet streams themselves, the characteristic of their flow pattern, and their continual circular path around Earth. This is another biblical confirmation that Earth is circular, not flat. The jet streams, including the polar jet stream around the South Pole, are also influenced by the sun and Earth's rotation. The jet streams are actually a balancing act, and it's not as simple as it looks. All of them work as a part of Earth's ecosystem.

> Jet streams are relatively narrow bands of strong wind in the upper levels of the atmosphere. The winds blow from west to east in jet streams but the flow often shifts to the north and south. Jet streams follow the boundaries between hot and cold air. ... The earth's rotation is responsible for the jet stream as well.[38]

The force (wind) that drives the climate and rain, and helps modulate the planet's temperature to sustain life, must be regulated. This balance cannot be left up to chance. The more we learn through science, the more fine-tuning we see. However, the Creator of the universe can certainly influence that which he created. Since he has power over Earth's entire ecological system, he can certainly cause seven years of plenty followed by seven years of drought, as Joseph proclaimed to Pharaoh, king of Egypt in the book of Genesis.

---

38   www.srh.noaa.gov/jetstream/global/jet.html

Evidence suggests the jet stream was at least partially responsible for the widespread drought conditions during the 1930s Dust Bowl in the Midwest United States. Normally, the jet stream flows east over the Gulf of Mexico and turns northward pulling up moisture and dumping rain onto the Great Plains. During the Dust Bowl, the jet stream weakened and changed course traveling farther south than normal. This starved the Great Plains and other areas of the Midwest of rainfall, causing extraordinary drought conditions.[39]

Paths of the Sea

The south polar jet stream that constantly circles the continent of Antarctica is not as affected by the sun as the other jet streams. It is one of the key components in keeping the continent frozen by keeping warm air out at higher and lower elevations, which is critical to the deep ocean nutrient-rich global conveyor belt also known as thermosaline circulations, because water density is dependent on temperature (thermo) and salinity (saline). In the Arctic region, salt water temperature is lowered to the point near freezing, which releases its salt. The released salt is absorbed by cold salt water below, making it denser. The increased salinity converts the salt water into brine, and the dense mixture falls to a lower level of the ocean. A constant current is created when the denser water sinks to the ocean floor and more water moves in to replace it. The replacement water goes through the same temperature and saline cycle, continuing the cycle, which also occurs in the north arctic region. Incredibly, this process drives a current of water around the globe from one polar region to the other. It is estimated to take a

---

39   Ibid.

thousand years to make the complete south/north circuit to feed the ocean creatures, including the critical base in the food chain, plankton.

> Thus saith the LORD, which *maketh* a way in the sea, and a path in the mighty waters. (Isaiah 43:16)

As God provides for land-based creation, he does the same for the ocean creatures. He created the path of the ocean currents. The ocean has both surface and deep underwater currents around the globe. The surface currents are created by the wind and are influenced directly by the sun and jet streams. God established the jet streams, like everything else. Their presence some twenty-five hundred years ago in the Bible tells us God knew their unique characteristic flows. If the ocean basins did not have the proper sloping elevation for the heavy brine to flow, it would just puddle where it cooled. God created the paths of the deep by creating the depths and mountains of the ocean floor through his control of plate tectonics around the globe—thus creating the means for the deep ocean currents to work. The use of the word "maketh" in this scripture correctly declares this is a continuous operation for the sustainer of life on Earth.

The North Atlantic undersea elevations on the southeastern coasts of Greenland and the Labrador Sea lend themselves to the flow of the cold, dense, salt-laden water that sinks to the depths. This is the main source for the deep, cold, flowing water of the conveyor belt of currents from the North. In the South, the flow comes from Antarctica, which is a strange and mysterious continent. It is considered a desert due to the low amount of snowfall it receives each year. The snow does not thaw, building constantly to an average elevation of 8,200 feet, the highest on any continent.

And yet, it has over three hundred lakes under the ice cap, which support a limited number of life forms that can survive without sunlight. Antarctica is comprised of several islands due to Earth's tectonic plate movements millions of years ago. It is in the ideal location to support life for the planet. Antarctica is a vital part of the transportation of the food chain via the conveyor belt of oceanic currents that affect all living things indirectly. A brine stream that flows into the depths of the sea, which originates at the Weddell Sea, alone is estimated to be about five hundred Niagara Falls in size, the largest continuous waterfall on Earth.

These deep ocean currents operate like the gravity-based plumbing systems we construct to carry waste material away from buildings. The key to the operation of land-based plumbing is the continual gradual downward slope of the piping. Mechanical pumping stations are placed in strategic locations to lift the waste product so the downward flow can continue toward its destination. The ocean currents require a similar grade for them to flow around the globe. In part through sea floor spreading, the Creator is making a path for the deep ocean currents by controlling the elevation of the ocean floor, facilitating the largest thermal plumbing operation on Earth. Where necessary, warm water at certain locations in the oceans causes upwelling, which lifts the cold water operating as lift stations along the deep ocean currents. The Creator is in control of the tectonic plates and subsea spreading and has set the location and elevation of the continents and bathymetry of the ocean floors for the dense brine and salt water mixture to flow around Earth. This must hold true for all the circuits to complete the journey from the polar regions to the oceans and back again on its thousand-year journey. (Bathymetry is the study of the beds or floors of water bodies, including the ocean, rivers, streams, and lakes. It has come to mean "submarine topography," or the depths and shapes of underwater terrain.)

Here is an example to illustrate the importance of the underwater terrain, as influenced by the movement of the tectonic plates and particularly the spreading of Earth and the magma that flows from it. The Mid-Atlantic Ridge is the most famous (and largest) underwater mountain range. It measures about ten thousand miles along the dark Atlantic Ocean floor. Oceanic ridges can vary greatly in elevation, from above sea level in Iceland to the depths of the Cayman Trench. Earth is full of such ridges. Other ridges around the world include the Pacific-Antarctic, East Pacific Rise, Chile Rise, Central Indian, Southeast Indian, Southwest Indian, Greenland-Iceland-Scotland, East Scotia, American-Antarctic, Nazca, Gakkel, Juan de Fuca, Gorda, Cocos, Aden, Explorer, and the Carlsberg Ridges. This is a large-scale elevation project by the Creator done in the total darkness of the deep oceans.

> Bathymetry influences ocean circulation both by steering large-scale flow and by influencing dissipation rates. This paper has reviewed examples of both types of processes. Because bathymetry blocks flow, it determines where ocean currents can go and where deep water can pass between basins. This in turn influences how rapidly heat can flow through the deep ocean. Rough topography also induces high vertical diffusivity, accelerating the vertical mixing of the ocean. This determines the stratification of the ocean and influences the penetration of heat and gases from the atmosphere into the deep ocean.[40]

---

[40] Sarah Gille and Stefan Smith, "Bathymetry and Ocean Circulation," *The GEBCO Project,* http://www.gebco.net/about_us/presentations_and_publications/documents/cen_conf_abstract_gille.pdf.

Increased genera follow all ten mass extinctions

Just as Jesus used the parable of the moral and helpful people as the preservers (salt) of the Earth, the actual salt in Earth's oceans preserves all life, playing a vital role in this life-giving cyclical current flow. Today, salt is plentiful and thus has become less valuable on the market. However, ocean salt is as important as ever, as it sustains the life of the creatures on the planet. The sun's heat, the moon, Earth's atmosphere, deep ocean currents, thermodynamics, and tectonic plates all play a harmonious score to sustain life on Earth, written and conducted by the great Creator of life.

> The fowl of the air, and the fish of the sea, and whatsoever passeth through the *paths of the seas*. (Psalm 8:8)

The words "paths" and "seas" can refer to the deep ocean currents that travel through every ocean and are interconnected to several different paths. The English word "paths" is the Hebrew word *orach* meaning "highways, frequented paths." This deep, underwater world is a mysterious, alien place void of light. Sunlight reaches only a few hundred feet below the water's surface; thus, 99 percent of the oceans' volume does not experience light. With no portable, waterproof lighting and breathing devices, the ancients could not investigate the ocean depths.

These currents carry heat, food, and oxygen like a conveyor throughout the planet. These currents were set originally and are changed by the changing movements of the continents, which the Creator has said he controls via the tectonic plates. These currents flow in the darkness of the deep oceans and ocean surfaces, influencing the weather.

The ocean currents (pathways) are extremely important to life on Earth. By keeping the ocean currents flowing, Earth and its creatures are supplied directly and indirectly with the proper percentage of oxygen needed for life. Scientists estimate 50 to 85 percent of the oxygen in Earth's atmosphere comes from tiny ocean plants called phytoplankton or microalgae, which live near the surface to get sunlight and are nourished in part by minerals from volcanic plumes carried by ocean currents. Like the plants on land, they produce oxygen through photosynthesis. The Sustainer uses sea floor spreading to feed the phytoplankton, which is the base food of several aquatic food webs. Jellyfish, snails, crustaceans, whales, and plant-eating sharks all benefit from the supply the Creator brought to their environment. The short-lived plankton requires a daily supply to sustain Earth's creatures with oxygen.

Atmospheric element levels are about 78 percent nitrogen, 21 percent oxygen, and 1 percent argon and other gases. The critical gas is oxygen. Oxygen levels below 19.5 percent at sea level are a warning of possible danger. This is just a guideline, as other gases and different atmospheric levels combined with the low oxygen level can create even more problems for humans. A high level of about 23 percent is not good for humans over a period of time either and can create some safety issues regarding combustion. My point is that the oxygen level of the atmosphere cannot be left to chance; it has to be precisely controlled. The problem is that humankind is unable to control it. This is a critical component of the balance of nature that cannot exist without a Sustainer with the power to manage oxygen levels and regulate other aspects of Earth's ecological system to maintain and protect life.

> Thus said God the Lord, he that created the heavens, and stretched them out; *he that spread forth Earth, and that which cometh out of it,* he that *giveth breath* unto the people upon it, and spirit to them that walk therein. (Isaiah 42:5)

Increased genera follow all ten mass extinctions

The God who continually gives breath to the people of Earth is also the architect of plate tectonics. He spreads the planet, as we witness with the mid-ocean ridges, where Earth's crust is literally spread open and the magma that flows creates the ocean floors. This same process helps to facilitate and regulate the carbon cycle, which has a major effect on Earth's climate. The tectonic plates help to remove carbon dioxide from the atmosphere, which regulates the makeup of the air we breathe. Just as the spreading forth of Earth is a continual process, so is the giving of breath. "Giveth breath" is a continuous action, not a reference to the original giving of life to Adam and Eve. The Creator/Sustainer controls the precipitation process, which controls plant life, which controls oxygen output to the planet to allow us to breathe.

> Thus saith the LORD, which giveth the sun for a light by day, and the ordinances of the moon and of the stars for a light by night, which *divideth the sea when the waves thereof roar;* The LORD of hosts is his name. (Jeremiah 31:35).

The Creator's hands are all over the operation of Earth, even controlling the tides and waves of Earth's oceans and seas with the moon, which has been assigned various ordinances that include stirring Earth's waters. The English word "divideth" is translated from the Hebrew word *raga*, which means "to stir up or disturb." This was written before Newton discovered the gravitational effects of the heavenly bodies, including the moon. Since Newton is correctly credited with the discovery of gravity for the heavenly bodies, the only other person who could have known about gravity, which is invisible, is the Creator himself. Earth is truly unique compared to the other heavenly bodies, as God predicted. It is no wonder the angels asked why God is so mindful of man. Considering all that

God has done and continues to do for us, humankind is indeed a special creation.

The Flood

Noah's flood is one of the most well-known events discussed by the Bible. After gaining an understanding of what the Creator said about the high elevation workings of the rain cycle, along with his hand in the movement of the tectonic plates in shaping and controlling the planet's surface, we can discuss the biblical flood. The Creator and Sustainer of the rain cycle and all its constituents could certainly cause an enormous amount of rain to fall on Earth or a given area, as happened during the flood in Noah's time. However, finding evidence of a global or local flood event in our dynamic and ever-changing planet has proven to be very difficult.

In light of all the scripture has said about creation, most of which has been affirmed, the Bible declares the flood did happen. The goal here is to provide evidence a global flood could have happened. However, the same evidence indicates a local flood was possible as well. One of the oldest arguments or questions about a global flood concerns the amount of water available to cover the entire planet. This is a legitimate concern because Earth is covered with approximately 70 percent water, and taking water from the oceans through the rain process to flood the remaining 30 percent of the land is sort of like chasing your shadow. Clearly, the amount of rain available would not be enough regardless of how long it lasted.

> In the six hundredth year of Noah's life, in the second month, the seventeenth day of the month, the same day were all the *fountains of the great deep* broken up, and the windows of heaven were opened. And the rain was upon Earth forty days and forty nights. (Genesis 7:11–12)

Increased genera follow all ten mass extinctions

When believers and unbelievers speak about Noah's flood, they often look at the forty days and forty nights of rain. As a resident of south Texas who was directly affected by the great flood brought by Hurricane Harvey to the Houston area over five days in 2017, I can appreciate what forty days of rain could do. A new appreciation of God's hand in the operation of Earth makes the feat of a global flood even more plausible. The amount of rain that can fall from the sky is truly mind-boggling. One inch of rain on one *acre* of land is 27,154 gallons of water, weighing 226,600 pounds, all of it floating in the clouds! Heavy rain can fall at a rate of two inches per hour. That is equal to 84,308 gallons of water for *each acre* of land per hour. The Creator can send 453,200 pounds of water (two inches) per acre via air mail and deliver it without destroying the delicate vegetation. For us to deliver that amount of water, it would take six, eighteen-wheeler tankers packing 75,533 pounds each per hour per acre.

As impressive as the rainfall may be, it seems to be a stretch to say that causing both the oceanic and atmospheric waters to fall to Earth would cause a global flood. It would certainly create some flooding, but to what extent? The fact that the Bible does not list this as the only cause must be recognized. The Creator's assertion of the additional source of water demonstrates knowledge of the amount of water on and in Earth.

First, the flood account describes the fountains of the great deep as its source of water before the second source of rain from above. To this day, the Creator continues to spread Earth's tectonic plates. This has been verified by the many mid-ocean ridges. At the appointed time in Noah's life, God opened *all of the fountains* of the great deep, implying there was more than one fountain.

We know about fresh water aquifers that have been tapped since ancient times for wells and today are used for agriculture. But the "fountains" here refer to deep sources, as the scripture proclaims. Job challenged God about his actions, and, in turn, God challenged Job about his ignorance of the secrets of the world he created.

In one of God's many statements about what he had done, God mentioned water hidden in rocks. Water in rocks is counterintuitive to normal thinking. Certainly, in Job's time, no one would have understood or believed that water was contained in rocks. These and other accurate scientific claims that were beyond the comprehension of the scribes must have come from a source of superior knowledge and understanding. That source is the author of the Bible, God.

> The waters are hid as with a stone, and the face of the deep is frozen. (Job 38:30)

The reference to a stone in the above verse is to an earthen stone, not to ice. In the original writing, the word "with" is not in the statement. The original writing reads "the waters are hid as a stone." According to scientific experiments, the water is within the ringwoodite stone. The scriptural reference to the face of the deep is not frozen, as we know ice to be. The word "frozen" is translated from the Hebrew word *lakad*, which means "to be seized or captured," just as the water is captured in the ringwoodite stone.

> The highwater storage capacity of minerals in Earth's mantle transition zone (410- to 660-kilometer depth) implies the possibility of a deep H_2O reservoir, which could cause dehydration melting of vertically flowing mantle. We examined the effects of downwelling from the transition zone into the lower mantle with high-pressure laboratory experiments, numerical modeling, and seismic P-to-S conversions recorded by a dense seismic array in North America. In experiments, the transition of hydrous ringwoodite to perovskite and (Mg,Fe)O produces

intergranular melt. Detections of abrupt decreases in seismic velocity where downwelling mantle is inferred are consistent with partial melt below 660 kilometers. These results suggest hydration of a large region of the transition zone and that dehydration melting may act to trap H_2O in the transition zone.[41]

I think we are finally seeing evidence for a whole-Earth water cycle, which may help explain the vast amount of liquid water on the surface of our habitable planet. Scientists have been looking for this missing deep water for decades." If just 1% of the weight of mantle rock located in the transition zone was water it would be equivalent to *nearly three times the amount of water in our oceans,* Jacobsen said. Jacobsen told the New Scientists that the hidden water might also act as a buffer for the oceans on the surface, explaining why they have stayed the same size for millions of years. "If [the stored water] wasn't there, it would be on the surface of Earth, and mountaintops would be the only land poking out," he said.[42]

Rare Diamond Confirms That Earth's Mantle Holds an Ocean's Worth of Water. The diamond contains ringwoodite, which is water-rich but only forms naturally under the extreme pressure found in Earth's mantle. "It's actually the confirmation that there is a very, very large amount of water that's trapped in a really distinct layer in the deep Earth,"

---

41   Schmandt, B., Jacobsen, S. D., Becker, T. W., Liu, Z., & Dueker, K. G. "Dehydration melting at the top of the lower mantle," *Science*, Vol. 334, issue 6189: 1265–1268
42   Guardian "Earth may have underground 'ocean' three times that on surface, https://www.theguardian.com/science/2014/jun/13/earth-may-have-underground-ocean-three-times-that-on-surface.

said Graham Pearson, lead study author and a geochemist at the University of Alberta in Canada.[43]

Theoretical scientists provide many out-of-the-box theories for the scientific community to pursue. However, Jacobsen and Pearson are *experimental* scientists. Jacobsen has worked on his project for decades, and these papers are based on that research. This is an example of the benefits of the scientific method. At the end of the process, Jacobsen's estimation of the flooded planet with land poking out resembles that of 2 Peter 3:5b, with Earth standing out of the water and in the water.

The fountains of the great deep *also* include the extremely high-pressure water found deep in the planet, as evidenced by the "dud wells" found in underground petroleum exploration. These are not the water wells that are drilled as a source of water for residential or commercial purposes, which require a pump to get the water to the surface. These very deep wells can only be drilled by deep petroleum-seeking equipment. Like many oil wells that are naturally pressurized, so are these dud wells of water, many exceeding ten thousand pounds per square inch. With the ability to create the stories of the atmosphere and create the needed components of the rain cycle, and given the overabundance of water in the Earth, no one can truthfully say a global flood is not plausible. God gave specific, scientifically verified information in the scripture on how he did it.

Whatsoever the LORD pleased, that did he in heaven, and in Earth, in the seas, and *all deep places.* (Psalm 135:6)

---

[43] Becky Oskin and Live Science, "Rare Diamond Confirms that Earth's Mantle Holds an Ocean's Worth of Water," *Scientific American*, http://easweb.eas.ualberta.ca/download/file/papers/paper_165.pdf.

Increased genera follow all ten mass extinctions

At the time of Noah's flood, the Creator actually ripped open the fountains of the deep, and the waters flowed. The size and scale of the flood is not described precisely. However, according to the estimate of the amount of water in the depths of Earth, it is substantial. Bringing this amount of water to the surface could mirror the original flooded condition of Genesis 1:2a: "And Earth was without form, and void; and darkness was *upon the face of the deep.*" At that time, before humans and other forms of life, the entire planet was flooded. This could reveal how the Creator caused the land to appear by driving the water deep beneath the planet's surface. Considering the aquifers, ringwoodite stone, and high-pressure, deep-water reservoirs, the Creator could cause the entire planet to flood without a drop of rain. He drives the divergent zones in Earth's tectonic plates to spread the oceans, and also drives the convergent zones that push the watery ocean crust down into the mantle. The movement of Earth's water is one of the changes this dynamic planet has undergone.

> Who led thee through that great and terrible wilderness, wherein were fiery serpents, and scorpions, and drought, where there was no water; who brought thee forth water out of the rock of flint. (Deuteronomy 8:15)

During the time of Israel's deliverance from slavery, we are told of the account of the miracle of bringing forth water from a rock. Science has shown that water can be obtained from a rock. After all the biblical descriptions of natural phenomena, which have confirmed by science, this seems like small potatoes. Those who have attempted to denigrate the Bible for proclaiming the various miracles God performed are minor complaints compared to the Creator's creation of an expanding, accelerating, and flat universe, along with controlling Earth's tectonic plates, establishing and maintaining the rain cycle, creating mass from that which cannot be seen, expanding Orion's belt, establishing the laws of physics, declaring the generations of the heavens and the heavenly hosts (galaxies), inducing mass extinctions and enabling a subsequent abundance of life, and so on and so on. To those who are skeptical of, or surprised by, Jesus walking on water and changing water into wine, welcome to the major league. The greatest natural miracle is the initial conditions of the first second creation biblical account of the universe. All of these descriptions in the Bible bring to light the name El-Shaddai, The Almighty.

> Knowing this first, that there *shall come* in the last days scoffers, walking after their own lusts, And saying, Where is the promise of his coming? for since the fathers fell asleep, all things continue as they were from the beginning of the creation. For this they willingly are ignorant of, that by the word of God the heavens were of old, and Earth standing out of the water and in the water: Whereby the world that then was, being overflowed with water, perished: But the heavens and Earth, which are now, by the same word are kept in store, reserved unto fire against the day of judgment and perdition of ungodly men. But, beloved, be not ignorant of this one thing, that one day is with the Lord as a thousand years, and a thousand years as one day. (2 Peter 3:3–8)

Verse three is a prophetic statement that places the intended audience at a later time than that of Peter, the author of this epistle. That later time is referred to as the last days. Based upon the predictions of the Bible, we are experiencing those last days. The skeptics will derisively refer to the account of Noah's flood as a biblical fairytale for the ignorant and uneducated. The "lusts" refer to their unbridled materialism. The Bible implies that the skeptics have the information needed to make an informed decision but ignore it. This is the willful ignorance that we see in our time.

The people of Peter's time could not have been willfully ignorant because they lacked the information we have today about the universe and Earth. They mock by proclaiming things will continue as they have from the beginning of creation. In other words, nothing outside of a natural source happened; there was no intervention by any entity since creation. At the time Peter was written, it was believed that the universe had always existed. Today, it is known that the universe had a beginning some 13.8 billion years ago. It is also known that our planet is over four billion years old and that a tremendous amount of water exists below Earth's surface.

Verse five states that at that time, Earth was standing out of the water and in the water, meaning the water did not cover higher elevations. The water caused all land-based living things to perish. There is no evidence that life existed before Genesis 1:2, the early formation of Earth. The same word or authority that maintains and sustains the universe is fully capable of changing it to cause whatever outcome the Creator desires.

I am fully persuaded the flood took place as the Bible proclaims. There is certainly nothing that can limit the capacity of the Creator in this or any other situation. However, I have not found any scripture or other evidence to make a convincing argument for either the global or local flood. But, since scripture does not give specifics, evidence is still needed to conclude whether the flood was local or global.

Chapter 7
Omni-God

The God of the Bible claims to have created the universe. There is evidence in this book that indicates he is the Creator. "Omni" means all, in all ways or places, without limits, etc. The God that created the universe has to be omni to accomplish such a feat. The word "universe" in this book means everything, i.e. excluding nothing. The descriptor omni, along with certain suffixes, is also used to describe certain attributes of the one who is all in all.

Omnipotent means all-powerful. The God of the Bible also claims he is almighty; he even makes this one of his names: El-Shaddai. The Creator must have more power than any power in the universe to be able to create and establish its operating laws and perimeters. This reflects his authority over the entire creation, and all subsequent authority is possessed by him. However, humankind is subject to time, the laws of physics, and many of the aspects of nature. Even in a limited role, humankind is capable of demonstrating the superiority of everything he creates using existing material. The nest is subject to the bird that created it. This holds true for all created things.

Omnipresent means to be present everywhere. The Creator of the Bible also claimed to be everywhere. David the Psalmist expressed his knowledge of God's presence.

> Whither shall I go from thy spirit? or whither shall I flee from thy presence? If I ascend up into heaven, thou art there: if I make my bed in hell, behold, thou art there. If I take the wings of the morning, and dwell in the uttermost parts of the sea; Even there shall thy hand lead me, and thy right hand shall hold me. (Psalms 139:7-10)

The Creator's omnipresence can be seen in his highest order in the natural universe: time. Time is the highest order because every natural thing is subject to it. Science knows it is impossible to conduct *any* experiment that excludes time and even space. Time and space are everywhere. The Omnipotent God who has all authority has extended a limited amount of it through time. Time, as an example of the extension of his authority, reaches everywhere with the absolute invisible power to keep all things moving in the *right* direction. That direction is called the arrow of time. The natural world is subject to the laws of physics; however, the laws of physics are all subject to the arrow of time.

Omniscient means all-knowing. The wisdom of God is reflected in the creation of everything: the universe. To know everything is necessary to create everything. Upon examination of what is known of the first billionth of a second after creation, with its low entropy, the structure of laws, established individual forces with extremely different strengths and character, perfectly flat space-time, extreme order and complexity, wisdom was before the creation event called the Big Bang. The universe we observe was determined within the first second of creation by the all-knowing Creator.

Increased genera follow all ten mass extinctions

An all-knowing Creator would know from the beginning what the end would be. This is evident in the first act of creation in the amount of energy used to create all things. Remember that all-natural existence came from, and is powered by, energy as reflected by the famous equation $E=mc^2$. This first act of imposing a finite amount of energy at creation, along with his establishment of the first and second law of thermodynamics, set in stone the eventual death of the universe.

The End of the Universe

The Bible talks about the creation of the universe, but does its eschatology or end reflect scientific observations? Consider again Isaiah 51:6, where we are commanded to gather natural evidence that will affirm the conditions: "Lift up your eyes to the heavens, and look upon the earth beneath," which states that the heavens will fade away like smoke, and the Earth will wear old like a garment. Looking upon the Earth, we observe a finite amount of fossil and nuclear fuel, as these reserves and other natural resources continue to dwindle in quantity. Looking to the heavens we find the expansion of the universe, accelerating while losing heat, currently at 2.7 degrees Kelvin, just as smoke dissipates and gets thinner as it rises. This statement in Isaiah demonstrates the all-knowing God knew this time would come. Furthermore, the Creator predicted a new heaven and Earth after the death of this current one.

For, behold, I create new heavens and a new Earth: and the *former shall not be remembered*, nor come into mind. (Isaiah 65:17)

For as the new heavens and the new Earth, which I will make, *shall remain before me,* saith the LORD, so shall your seed and your name remain. (Isaiah 66:22)

And I saw a new heaven and a new Earth: for the first heaven and the *first Earth were passed away*; and there was *no more sea*. (Revelation 21:1)

First, I want to point out the use of the phrase heaven and Earth in all three passages. This is the same phase used in Genesis 1:1, which means all of creation or the universe. All of them have the same meaning. A new universe is what is predicted here, while Isaiah declared this universe will not be remembered, and the next one shall remain before the Creator. Revelation also speaks of this heaven and Earth as passing away, and it ends with an interesting caveat: there will be no more sea or water. It seems as if during Earth's passing, it lost its water. What would cause such a thing? In the fourth eon (day) of the Genesis account, our sun had grown to the Goldilocks conditions needed for life on Earth as acknowledged by the Creator. The sun is still in what is considered its main sequence. However, the sequence does not stop at the four-billion-year midlife point of the sun. The heat of the sun's later stage is estimated to be 40 percent greater than today. That level of heat will cause all the water on Earth to boil away into outer space, leaving the Earth with no more seas. In time, the sun will continue to expand to a red giant star that will engulf the Earth and bring another scripture into focus.

But the day of the Lord will come as a thief in the night; in the which the heavens shall pass away with a great noise, and the *elements shall melt with fervent heat,* the Earth also and the works that are therein shall be burned up. (2 Peter 3:10)

Increased genera follow all ten mass extinctions

The use of "day" in Genesis chapter one signifies a variety of time frames. The same holds true here in 2 Peter 3:10, compared with other scriptures that use this phrase, where day means a particular time, not a duration of time. The day of the Lord is not the same as the similar phase in Zechariah 14:1 or 1 Thessalonians 5:2 which references a particular time where God will take action against the ungodly. The thief in the night in both scriptures is a reference to an action taken by God at an unknown time.

Here in 2 Peter, "heavens" is not used in a combination phase of "heavens and Earth" as in other scripture which refer to the universe. Here the single reference to the heavens is to the layers of Earth's atmosphere. The word "elements" means the rudiments of the atmosphere, which is about 78 percent nitrogen and 21 percent oxygen, making it a nonflammable mixture. The fact that all the lightning, nuclear reactions, rocket and jet engines, etc. do not ignite the atmosphere has demonstrated it is not capable of spontaneous combustion. In order for it to burn as this scripture proclaims, it must be subjected to a continual, extremely large, and hot external self-generating source like the sun, i.e. fervent heat. To be all-knowing required knowing the future, proving God is not subject to any part of time.

Many theologians consider 2 Peter 3:10 to mean a renovated Earth. I consider it a totally new Earth because the scripture makes one statement that the atmosphere, Earth, and the works of man all shall be consumed by fire. If the Earth is to be renovated, all three will be renovated. In addition, verse eleven again summarizes the fate of the atmosphere, Earth, and works on it (all) with a slightly different wording: "All these things shall be dissolved." The Greek word *luo*, translated as "dissolved" in verse eleven, continues describing the destruction of the non-combustible atmosphere in a state of being on fire from an external source. Verse thirteen affirms the destruction with the promise of a new heavens and Earth, which compares with Revelation 21:1. Our sun, like other stars its size and composition that have run out of it fuel, will die with an explosion generating great noise and devolve into a planetary nebula and, finally, a white dwarf star.

> And as he sat upon the mount of Olives, the disciples came unto him privately, saying, tell us, when shall these things be? and what shall be the sign of thy coming, and of *the end of the world?* (Matthew 34:3)

The disciples asked Jesus on the mount of Olives three big questions in which they were concerned. It was good for them to ask questions to get answers. Jesus did not rebuke them for a lack of faith; he understood that knowledge strengthens faith. He in turn answered all three questions in the verses following. He answered the question concerning the end of the world in a concise manner in verse thirty-five.

> *Heaven and earth shall pass away,* but my words shall not pass away. (Matthew 24:35)

The all-knowing God demonstrates he is not limited by time, predicting the future end of the Earth and sun; even the universe in other scriptures!

Evil

Many object to God's "omni" claim due to the existence of evil. God certainly knows of all the evil and has the power to set any structure for the creation. The existence of evil doesn't negate the possibility of the existence of God. A philosophical question often presented by atheists is that if God is omnibenevolent, or all good, why is there evil? It is necessary to know the concept of omnibenevolence is a religious concept, not a proclamation of the author of the Bible. God claimed to be omnipotent, omnipresent, and omniscient; he did not claim to be *all* good in accordance with our perspectives. He is certainly a benevolent God; however, he does not limit himself to the various human concepts of benevolence; he's also a God of judgment and wrath. As Creator, he is all-powerful, all-knowing, and operates everywhere. So, why is there evil? Moral evil is part of the free will granted to humankind by God. There must be a legitimate choice with equal, legitimate consequences to be legitimate free will. This choice is the concept of binary opposites giving meaning to one another. Examples are hot and cold, up and down, and good and evil. This authority to choose is what makes humans free will agents.

The question of evil generally compares the total evil observed in the world with a hypothetical absence of evil. Thus, any non-zero amount of evil implies an evil God. Contrary to this assertion, according to the Bible's account of the beginning of humanity, we find an extremely *unbalanced* choice that God presented to Adam and Eve. Specifically, they could choose between eating the fruit of a copious number of trees whose fruit was permitted, representing obedience, or one forbidden tree, which represented disobedience. The command to Adam from the Creator is not to the tree of evil as some mistakenly purport. The forbidden tree and its single fruit contain the knowledge of *both* good and evil. Based upon the deceptive counsel of Satan, the first couple determined the forbidden fruit would make them wise, thus discounting God's counsel. After eating of the fruit of the tree, Adam and Eve came to know both good and evil, which says they could not fully know good without evil. The Creator embodied both good and evil in a single fruit from a single tree. They existed in a good environment in the garden with limited knowledge. They used their limited knowledge along with misguided advice not to trust God. God's intent and authority were questioned based on the premise that he was depriving them of an elevated state through this hidden treasure of knowledge. The promised separation (death) from God indeed happened, as God had previously warned Adam. The first couple's choice not to follow God demonstrates the capacity of free will to determine their fate with full consequences. All humanity has been granted the same freedom of choice to follow God's moral ways.

> And the LORD God said, Behold, the man is *become* as one of us, to know good *and* evil: (Genesis 3:22a)

If eaten, the tree of life would have allowed Adam and Eve to live forever. In spite of the fact that free will was tilted toward good by the available choices, they made *two* bad decisions. The first bad choice was not to eat of the tree of life. This indicates their limited knowledge of what was good. Of course, the second bad choice was to disobey God and to eat of the forbidden fruit. This brought about the knowledge of both good and evil to Adam and Eve. The decisions of humans today still bring about both good and evil. As ruler of the Earth, Adam was to follow the laws of operation set by God. Adam's dominion was limited to Earth. So, the effect of his sin was also limited to Earth. Adam could not extend the effects of death to the universe, as he had no authority beyond Earth. The universe and God's angels, which are also creatures, had already experienced the fall of Lucifer's followers and the death of the stars. The genuine free will in heaven also allowed evil.

The concept of seed and fruit multiplication in the reproduction of plants and animals established by the Creator also extends to the moral law, often termed "sowing and reaping." This law also applies equally to both evil and good. From the initial seeds of good and evil, many generations later, humankind has planted more and more seed, which has resulted in bumper crops. God gave us legitimate free will with the capacity to do good and evil. Much of the evil that is attributed to God is that of humans. Humans are responsible for both the humane and inhumane acts of history. We want God to limit our capacity to do evil and not limit our capacity to do good. The authority to choose brings the capacity to carry out that choice. Having the capacity to do good comes with the capacity to do evil.

The physical laws are immutable and the physical world has to operate within that authority. The physical laws are established by the Creator of the natural universe. The moral laws are just as legitimate, immutable, and established by the same Creator. Both these categories of laws have cause and effect actions, which make them laws. The cause and effect of the physical laws are generally immediate. The moral laws can take some time to see the effects.

> Because sentence against an evil work is not executed speedily, therefore the heart of the sons of men is fully set in them to do evil. (Ecclesiastes 8:11)

Humans live by an apparent underlying "moral standard." This standard is shown even in war, when we expect the enemy not to destroy hospitals, take part in crimes against humanity, or commit genocide. Where did this moral standard come from? Adam and Eve experienced good in the garden before they fully knew what good was. First came life; only after life is death possible. The same holds true for love and emotional hurt. This is a phenomenon most have experienced, whether atheist or theist. The degree of emotional hurt upon the loss of a loved one depends upon the degree of love in the relationship. The loss of a dear and close uncle hurts more than a distant uncle. If love was not first established, there is little or no emotional hurt. A personal, deep-rooted love yields a proportionally deep hurt when love is lost, not only to death, but in separation. When law enforcement encounters a homicide in which the victim has been violently murdered, they often surmise that the suspect had a personal relationship with the victim. This is a classic case of good gone bad. Bad or evil is not a sign that God does not exist; it is an affirmation that the standard of love and good exists.

The criminal laws take into account one's ability to reason between "right and wrong." The verdict of a jury of "not guilty by reason of insanity" implies the person's mental capacity is below the threshold of genuine knowledge of right or wrong.

Nature does not establish such moral standards as demonstrated in what we call the food chain, where the lion and countless other carnivores continually kill to feed their babies. For the human mother to feed her babies is good. However, in the animal kingdom, a mother must kill, sometimes even kill the babies of others, to feed her own. How can both situations be "good?" Who is the authority to impose such an opposing standard of good? Nature has no moral code. Observation of the animal kingdom reveals they gather in groups but there is no religious activity. Among primates, there is the head male, but no priest. We find the queen bee within the hive, but no priest. These demonstrate order, but it is an order without morality.

If all creation were only nature, humans would be like *all* the other creatures. Humans are the only creatures that have a moral compass. To recognize moral or natural evil is to recognize a moral standard that is not from nature. Only an intellectual creature with an innate moral compass has the ability to recognize good, evil, and a Creator who established it.

If pain is considered an evil, it is a necessary one; it helps to guide us away from actions that are destructive to our well-being. For example, pain in our body helps protect us from destroying the body by informing us that something is wrong. It can vary from slightly wrong with a small pain to very wrong with great pain. The pain of a twisted ankle will force restricted use until the pain subsides and the ankle heals so that it can be used normally again. Although unpleasant, pain actually extends our life span. It would be difficult to grow to adulthood without pain; and if we lived that long, the broken bones and other damaged parts would greatly limit our ability to accomplish simple tasks.

Pain in society is analogous to our body in that is shows us that something is wrong in an area demanding attention and action to both stop what is causing the pain, along with allowing it to heal. Various social pains can signal to humankind that something is wrong when something destructive or evil is occurring. No one likes pain or evil, but they have beneficial contributions to a society. Seeking to destroy religion does not help the problem of evil.

Natural evil is considered to come from that which humans have no influence or control over, like earthquakes, tornadoes, and other natural disasters. The Bible claims God created and controls the atmosphere, which brings about storms and natural phenomena as discussed earlier in this book: the jet streams, rain, lightning, tornadoes, and whirlwinds. The Bible claims God is in control of the tectonic plates, which are the source of earthquakes and volcanoes. Like the abundance of evil implied by the question of moral evil, the question of natural evil has the same implication. According to the atheist, the great natural evil that causes death and injury can only be from God. To imply God is responsible for natural evil also implies he is indeed the Creator and Sustainer of this universe. However, the damage and benefits must be examined.

According to the U.S. National Weather Service, in 2014 (the latest available data at the writing of this book), in the United States, Puerto Rico, Guam, and the Virgin Islands, 388 people died and 2,203 were injured as a result of lightning, tornadoes, thunderstorm wind, hail, cold, heat, flash flood, river flood, coastal storm, tsunami, rip currents, hurricanes, winter storms, ice, avalanche, drought, dust storm, dust devil, rain, fog, high wind, waterspout, fire weather, mudslide, volcanic ash, and miscellaneous causes. These are not just numbers; they are 388 lives lost. It is just a tragic as a passenger jet crash.

Let's compare the 388 deaths from natural evil attributed to the Sustainer's operation with the transportation system, also used to sustain life and the economy. Man designed the highways and vehicles along with the laws that govern them and granted the free will for humans to use it; God had no hand in it. According to the National Highway Traffic Safety Administration, auto accidents caused 32,675 deaths and 2,300,000 injuries in 2014. And yet, the transportation system is not considered to be evil, and rightly so. The system produces tremendous benefits for the economy and the citizenry. The system is also a lot safer than it once was. With targeted safety efforts by automobile manufacturers, highway design, and law enforcement, the annual fatality rate has been reduced from over fifty thousand per year in earlier years. Tens of thousands of lives are saved annually by these safety efforts. Man has the knowledge and power to stop the entire operation and revert back to the horse and buggy days.

So, why are *only* God's beneficial natural operations considered evil? Neither of these two operations should be considered evil; but if one is evil, both are evil. And if man's operation is evil, we all participate in that evil with the individual free will not to contribute. Seeing the numbers behind the argument, God is not the evil villain he is portrayed to be.

The price of free will is indeed very high. The suffering and death due to diseases like cancer can be devastating. God is the Creator of life and limits its duration. Aging is a design of God. If the natural life on Earth is considered the full extinct of our existence, the suffering in this 'life' can weigh heavy on the evil side. However, the Creator created humankind to live eternally, which changes the total relative impact of evil experience on that existence compared to an average natural life of eighty years. The difficulties in life are real and affect the innocent, righteous, unbelievers, and believers. No one is immune. God indeed allows suffering in this natural part of life. The God who predicted all these natural phenomena in the Bible, including an expanding and accelerating universe, also predicted a life hereafter.

The Bible is not just some holy book; it is the word of the Creator, God. In spite of the suffering, there is genuine hope. However, if your worldview is exclusively natural, there is no hope after death.

Humankind engages in self-inflicting suffering and death. Man has created a product that adds zero benefits to society and yet it destroys countless lives and families. That product is tobacco in its many forms. More than twenty million Americans have died as a result of smoking since the first Surgeon General's report on smoking and health was released in 1964. Cigarette smoking causes more than 480,000 deaths *annually* in the United States.[44] It causes about one in every five deaths in the United States, all preventable. More than sixteen million Americans are currently living with a disease caused by smoking.[45]

Alcohol, another man-made product, adds an additional eighty thousand fatalities annually. Collectively, man can stop all this pain and suffering, but the Creator grants people the free will to decide to use these products, even knowing it hurts the one making the personal choice and the countless others who are innocent.

God allows suffering among humans and the animal world. The Bible is open concerning this issue. The very redemption of man from the state of moral evil comes through the suffering of Jesus Christ. Immediately before the crucifixion, Jesus prayed for an alternative way other than the particular cup of suffering God

---

[44] 2014 Surgeon General's Report: The Health Consequences of Smoking—50 Years of Progress, Executive Summary; 1.
[45] Centers for Disease Control and Prevention, http://www.cdc.gov/tobacco/data_statistics/fact_sheets/fast_facts/

was requiring. God's answer was that Jesus must go through that suffering to bring about redemption to mankind. Suffering is a part of God's plan; it does not negate his existence. No man can really answer on his behalf. Our personal preferences and opinions are not the benchmark to measure the Creator. The method and timing of removing evil and suffering from mankind are the purview of the Creator. He is capable of creating the magnificent universe; he will also take care of evil and suffering by his own method and at a time of his choosing. His descriptions about the creation of the natural world are on point, and I trust he will complete the task of eliminating moral evil and natural suffering according to his method and timing. His promises have always proven to be true. So, too, will this one.

The Unknown God

Without the use of instruments and with only limited knowledge of science and the way nature works, the ancients attributed natural phenomena to a variety of deities. The Egyptian deity Ra was the sun god. The Greek deity Zeus was the god of the sky. Many people today ridicule the ancients as being ignorant and unlearned for attributing unknown natural phenomena to the hand of gods. I think by doing so, they show irreverence toward those from whom the accumulated knowledge we are all taught came. During the process of accumulating knowledge as a civilization, mistakes were made; however, we all stand on the shoulders of our ancestors.

Ironically, those who belittle the ancients are often guilty of the same infraction. Unbeknown to most, science itself has come full circle to attribute everything we know and don't know to another great god—Nature. By all the accolades, credits, intellect, power to establish laws and evolutionary choices given to Nature, it seems to be the entity behind the curtain, as in the Wizard of Oz; making things happen and controlling what is occurring on the stage of the universe. Naturalists assert that Nature established the law of physics, time, and space, and created life. Nature is said to be hiding its secrets from us, making discovery so difficult to ascertain. According to them, it is Nature that created the stars and galaxies. It is often said, "It is Nature's way of doing things." Considering the sum of all that is attributed to Nature, having power over all things natural, it has the character of a deity. Ironically, those who deny the God of the Bible, have a god of their own. By inference, Nature is omnipotent and all-powerful, able to establish and change anything in the universe. By inference, Nature is omnipresent, having natural authority both locally and throughout the universe. And by inference, Nature is also omniscient, all-knowing.

One of the main criticisms about God is that he is invisible. If he is God, they say, he would show himself in the method of their choice. Strangely, no one seems to have the same complaints about Nature. Nature is like dark matter, natural in essence but invisible. Why are those who believe in the invisible God of the Bible perceived as unintelligent and those who believe in the invisible Nature are the thinkers? Also, if Nature created the universe, where did Nature come from? Does this question sound familiar? And, if we can't tell where Nature came from, we should not accept anything attributed to it. Nature is their God of the gaps. Whenever a gap in knowledge is encountered about how the universe works, Nature is inserted as the answer.

As the Bible states, there is nothing new under the sun. An account in the New Testament is similar to this situation, where the Apostle Paul encountered certain Stoic and Epicurean philosophers in Athens. Just as the philosophers of Paul's time made a shrine to the unknown god, many today have done the exact thing for Nature, their unknown god. Their devotion to Nature is easy to behold. Like our ancestors, unknown phenomena are attributed to the unknown god, Nature.

> For as I passed by, and beheld your devotions, I found an altar with this inscription, TO THE UNKNOWN GOD. *Whom therefore ye ignorantly worship*, him declare I unto you. God that made the world and all things therein, seeing that he is Lord of heaven and Earth, (Acts 17:23–24)

Before the Bible was written, Nature was the first "book" or reference to the God of the universe. This is not a new term or reference for he who calls himself Creator. Over six thousand years ago, it was embodied in the introduction of himself to humankind in the Bible: "In the beginning, God created the heaven and Earth." Thus, his introduction is not to the spiritual or metaphysical world but to that which can be seen and touched, to help humans understand the capacity and power of their Creator. From the creation of humankind to the time of the Exodus of Israel from Egypt, no Bible existed. God revealed himself through direct revelation and nature. And nature still plays a large part in his special and general revelation today. He directs us to the heavens to look for his glory and revelation in the Book of Psalms. He has spoken through nature to all humankind irrespective of the era, language, or education of the individual. He continues today even more in light of new discoveries.

> The heavens declare the glory of God; and the firmament sheweth his handywork. Day unto day uttereth speech, and night unto night sheweth knowledge. There is no speech nor language, where their voice is not heard. (Psalm 19:1–3)

> For when the Gentiles, which have not the law, do by nature the things contained in the law, these, having not the law, are a law unto themselves. (Romans 2:14)

Increased genera follow all ten mass extinctions

The scripture above from the Book of Romans shows that the nature factor is still in effect today. Nature includes the works of his hands and represents his desires. God uses nature as part of the structure of his moral laws. This is for those who have never read or seen the Bible and those who lived before the Bible was written.

From ancient times to today, humankind has conjured up various cosmological theories pertaining to the origin of the universe based on religion, philosophy, folklore, and science. Throughout the ages, these myths, demigods, and theories have been either affirmed or disproven with our growing yet limited knowledge and understanding of the workings of the universe. During those ancient times, in the backdrop of all the chatter and confusion, arose a revelation of himself, a deity who was unwilling to share any glory, power, or majesty with any other god, entity, or creature. In fact, he claimed to be the only God, being the only Creator. As time passed, many gods were thought to be generated by the thoughts and desires of humankind to appease their ideas and perceptions. To the dismay of many who think God is just one more myth produced by ancient religion, his influence continues to grow among the world's population despite the great wealth of knowledge we have obtained. Having a worldview limited as if by horse blinders, some have gone so far as to declare God to be a delusion, unnecessary, and even dead. As Mark Twain was mistaken for his seriously ill cousin and publicly reported to be dead (an event that led Twain to declare news of his death had been "a great exaggeration"), don't mistake the God of the Bible to be one of those fallen myths. This is a revelation to many; the unknown god, a.k.a. Nature, is the God of the Bible. So, when Nature is referenced, God is glorified. As the Apostle Paul declared to the philosophers in Athens, "him declare I unto you."

Faith

> Now faith is the *substance* of things hoped for, the evidence of things not seen. (Hebrews 11:1)

The first thing that is apparent about this scripture is that faith requires substance or a foundation. Faith contains hope; however, hope without substance is just that—hope. Faith requires evidence. Hope requires nothing but a desire or a wish. If a foundation for belief is not there, we should identify the notion or desire as hope. Hope coupled with a foundation is faith.

Consider this parable: The champion professional heavyweight boxer is in a boxing ring with a twelve-year-old boy. The only weapons they have are their fists. If we desire the boy to win the battle, it is mere hope, because there is no reasonable foundation on which to base our belief that he can overcome the champ. However, based on the champ's experience, strength, size, and ability to take punches from other professionals, never mind from a boy, we have a solid foundation on which to base our belief that he will win. Regardless of our hope for the boy to overcome, there is no reason he should. Based on knowledge, we have faith the champ will win.

> Lift up your eyes on high, and behold who hath created these things, that bringeth out their host by number. (Isaiah 40:26a)

> Lift up your eyes to the heavens, and look upon Earth beneath: for the heavens shall vanish away like smoke, and Earth shall wax old like a garment. (Isaiah 51:6a)

Increased genera follow all ten mass extinctions

The Bible admonishes us to investigate the heavens, even Earth, to verify God as Creator and the things he promised pertaining to Earth. This is certainly not the blind faith alleged by those who are ignorant of the Bible. The very command to examine the heaven and Earth implies there is evidence to make a reasonable conclusion about who is Creator. Empirical scientific evidence, compared to an accurate time-based record of God's biblical claims, along with reason, are the only tools needed in this modern time of great scientific knowledge. In the midst of this chatter about blind faith is the lack of understanding of what constitutes faith. The Bible gives an informed, accurate definition of faith.

Faith is not exclusively a religious concept. The same holds true for science. When theories are presented for consideration, peers examine the facts against the theory. The word "faith" is not the word of choice in this field. The more "out of the box" the theory, the less faith the scientific community has in it. When the theory is successfully subjected to testing by more and more scientists and measured against the laws of physics, communicated by mathematics, confidence in the theory grows. The reverse happens when the theory does not conform to the laws of physics or cannot be demonstrated mathematically. This confidence is based upon the laws and is the substance that supports the hope that the theory is true. Successful experiments and observations increase faith to a point of limited knowledge. Eventually, it will move from a hypothesis to a theory to become what is known by science.

God has dealt to every man the measure of faith. (Romans 12:3b)

A progressive manifestation of authority has been made by God throughout the history of the Bible, from Noah and Abraham until today. In Noah's time, God demonstrated his authority to bring judgment by nature to mankind, foretold in the building of the ark. In Abraham's time, God demonstrated to Abram and Sarai he is greater than time by predicting a nation would proceed from their union. God waited after both passed their reproductive ages to revive what was dead, and Isaac was born. In addition, God predicted both sons would be fathers of a nation. Isaac, in particular, would go in captivity and after four hundred years, God would free them. Over the predicted time, the relationship between Israel and Egypt turned for the worse. God delivered the fledgling nation by a man called Moses armed with a staff. The deliverance was done in a fashion that demonstrated God's authority over the greatest nation and nature. The demonstration of power provided the basis for the faith he asks Israel and other nations to have in the *living* God. For hundreds of years, this was the relatively current reference to God's authority. This establishment of authority was for the people of that time to challenge God's demonstration of power.

Later in Bible history, God demonstrates his authority over time itself, and the nations, through the prophet Jeremiah to predict the Babylonian captivity of the disobedient chosen nation of Israel, along with its duration of seventy years. During the promised captivity, God predicted through a dream of King Nebuchadnezzar of Babylon the rise and fall of the coming great kingdoms. History shows the king's dream was correctly revealed to Daniel in a night vision immediately thereafter. The kingdoms came to pass in the order God predicted: the Babylonian Empire, followed by the Medo-Persian Empire, Greek Empire (to be split into four parts which occurred after the death of Alexander the Great), and the Roman Empire. During the time of this prophetic fulfillment, the people experienced the authority of God's knowledge of the future and control of the nations. This divine activity bridged the time of the Bible's four hundred years of silence between the Old and New Testaments; this faith substance was added to the previous substance, until the time of Jesus when Israel was under the rule of the predicted Roman Empire. Just as in early biblical time, during this time period humankind experienced the life and work of Jesus, the greatest work of God. His life, death and resurrection were easily challengeable at the time; they now can only be historically affirmed. The coming of Jesus added more substance for humanity to believe in Bible prophecy.

The Old Testament authority is carried into the New Testament by way of the many prophecies concerning the promised Savior. That Savior is Jesus. There were so many distinct prophecies concerning him, he could not claim to be the Messiah with mere words of wisdom. The following are events foretold over four hundred years before being fulfilled in Jesus, events which are totally out of his control: born in Bethlehem, born of a virgin, seed of David, not a bone of him broken, suffered outside the camp, crucified at Passover, hanged on a tree, would not see corruption, given vinegar in thirst, gave his back to those who smote him, plucked off the hair of his face, face spat upon, scourged, judged, found innocent, killed, buried with the rich, died before temple and Jerusalem destroyed, sold for thirty pieces of silver, and he would conquer death. Thereby, more substance was added to the foundation of faith.

The Old Testament becomes more authoritative by divinely determining future events while Jesus's claim to be the Messiah is validated by matching the predicted authoritative word of God. In addition to those events outside of his control, Jesus followed the example of God in demonstrating in natural ways that he is greater than nature. Jesus did not ask the people of his time to just believe in him because of his words. By changing the water into wine, walking on water, commanding the storm to cease, raising the dead, replacing the severed ear, opening the eyes of one born blind, ascension into heaven, the resurrection, and many other miracles, he demonstrates the supernatural. After the resurrection, Jesus did not disappear but made himself known to the people of the area for forty days. The people of the time were given the opportunity to affirm his authenticity. Additional substance was added to the foundation of faith. Many skeptics today proclaim the Bible is not true because these and other events cannot be confirmed today (according to their methods). History is the only way to affirm events of the past. Throughout history, the people of that time were to determine the truth of God's word based upon his actions of their era.

Today, history holds true as God reveals his hand in the predictions of the Bible, confirmed by current observations. All humankind from the very beginning has known humans cannot know the future. The multiplying of knowledge and travel to and fro were predicted by the Bible thousands of years ago in the Book of Daniel. The travel from one part of the Earth to another has become commonplace. The multiplying of knowledge is evident from the Industrial Revolution to the golden age of scientific knowledge and the exponential growth of computing capacity. In an effort to eliminate God from the narrative of creation, some have attempted to use the new discoveries of science to imply there is no need for God. With further discoveries in science, the same rhetoric has escalated. But God has flipped the script; new discoveries in science have increasingly shown in the last one hundred years the author of the Bible is indeed the Creator of the universe. This is one of the greatest opportunities for the Creator to show he is greater than time and the universe. He has turned what was used to try to bury him and has co-opted it to raise his power and authority to yet a higher level.

Empirical evidence from the scientific methods of experiment and observation has confirmed the Bible's statements concerning Earth and the universe. These statements certainly did not come from the scribes' own minds, because they were from a pre-scientific era. Only by divine revelation were these truths declared, which adds creditability to God's sovereign authority reflected in the Bible.

Increased genera follow all ten mass extinctions

Today, as during all the previous biblical eras, God has manifested himself in various ways. Of course, individual experiences and manifestations have always occurred. The latest and most enduring manifestation for humanity is that of Jesus. Now, we can understand scientifically the majestic phenomena that demonstrate the power and authority of the Creator of the universe. Consider all the various allusions in the Bible to all the natural things which can be seen even though they are made from that which cannot be seen (elementary particles), even with a microscope of any kind—all confirmed by scientific evidence. As in generations past, the generation of today has a strong foundation of faith to believe other proclamations of the entire Bible. We are without excuse. By examining the Bible as a book of history against its creative claims has added to its authority. There is no other book that has outlined the aspects of the universe from the beginning to its end as the Bible.

Amen

Through the creative and sustaining journey within the Bible of the works of God, this book has examined scriptures by twenty scribes from twenty-eight of the sixty-six books of the King James canon over a 1500-year period of time. The King James Version of the Bible is used in this book because it is a formal equivalence (word for word) translation. This 1611 AD translation cannot be considered slanted to mirror science. How could this many scientifically uneducated scribes living so many centuries ago contribute such an accurate scientific-biblical account of creation, from the first second to the future end of the universe? Only through divine revelation could these phenomena be described by Bronze and Iron Age scribes. This testimony affirms God as Creator and the Bible as the divine revelation of God himself!

Most of the major phenomena of our universe were described by the Bible long before they were discovered by science, such as the beginning of the universe, the expansion, acceleration, and flatness of the universe, unseen mass, dark matter, dark energy, space, the Higgs field, early Earth formation, plate tectonics, deep ocean currents, layers of the atmosphere, jet streams, and others.

> But thou, O Daniel, shut up the words, and seal the book, even to the time of the end: many shall run to and fro, and knowledge shall be increased. (Daniel 12:4)

Humans continue to learn more and more about the universe in which they live—they continue to decipher the messages the Creator has placed throughout the Bible. This knowledge drives us forward. An exponential increase of knowledge of energy sparked the Industrial Revolution of the eighteenth and nineteenth centuries, which set the course of the modern era defined by knowledge and management of information. The twentieth and twenty-first centuries have been the golden age of physics and cosmology, yielding massive discoveries of the working of our universe. The Bible ironically predicted this abundance of knowledge, and ironically, this knowledge has been used by many in the scientific community to discredit the Bible. While mere mortals, some have gone as far as to authorize themselves as the universe's coroner by declaring God dead. God has turned the attempted derision to his triumph. Due to the abundance of knowledge, the myth that the Bible contains no evidence of God and creation has been busted.

This is no "God of the gaps" argument and no need to find celestial teapots orbiting somewhere in space; the evidence is supplied by the Creator to support his own existence. Some of the knowledge of creation in the Bible is hidden, scattered throughout in plain sight in the form of metaphors. It is the work of this book to gather these creation metaphors and arrange them in chronological order as it relates to the natural creation. The Creator had to wait until man discovered his secrets of creation through science, and then the metaphors he used in the Bible to declare these phenomena became clearer in time. The metaphor of laying out a tent in which to dwell became comprehensible only after the discovery that the fabric of space-time is flat. These secrets do not exclusively belong

Increased genera follow all ten mass extinctions to the scientific community. Just as God commanded us to look to the heavens to see who created these, he also declared the secrets he reveals belong to all.

> The secret things belong unto the LORD our God: but those things which are revealed belong unto us and to our children forever... (Deuteronomy 29:29)

Not only do these revealed secrets belong to us, we are encouraged to pass this knowledge on to the next generation and the one after that. The latest scientific discoveries are indeed "good news" (gospel) signifying the continued work of God as Creator. Based upon these scientific affirmations of the creation claims, the authority of the Bible has been enhanced. As Creator, God is the final authority in all matters in the universe he created. He is the one and only God.

> Lift up your eyes on high, and behold who hath created these things. (Isaiah 40:26a)

After hundreds of years of looking and studying the heavens, with the aid of powerful complex telescopes and instruments, the Bible has proven to be the divine words of the Creator and Sustainer of this universe, the God of Abraham, Isaac, and Jacob, the Almighty.

> I am Alpha and Omega, the beginning and the ending, saith the Lord, which is, and which was, and which is to come, the Almighty. (Revelation 1:8)

www.ingramcontent.com/pod-product-compliance
Lightning Source LLC
Chambersburg PA
CBHW070557100426
42744CB00006B/313